Ready-to-Go

Super Book of Outline Maps

SCHOLASTIC
PROFESSIONAL BOOKS

New York • Toronto • London • Auckland • Sydney
Mexico City • New Delhi • Hong Kong

Cover design by Norma Ortiz
Interior design by Norma Ortiz
Maps by Mapquest.com

ISBN 0-439-11761-5

Table of Contents

Introduction

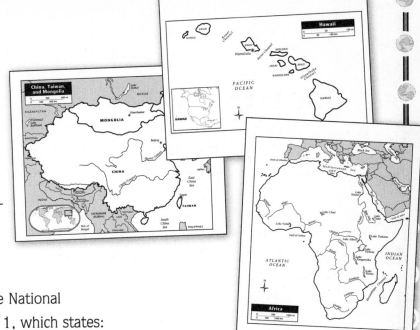

The outline maps in this book are an instant way for you to help your students become geography-wise. You simply reproduce the maps, and you and your students are ready to use them in reports, for bulletin-board displays, and for all kinds of activities and projects.

Using the maps will also help you to meet the National Geography Standards, in particular, Standard 1, which states:

The geographically informed person knows and understands:

Knowledge Standard I – How to use maps and other geographic representations, tools, and technologies to acquire, process, and report information from a spatial perspective.

Supply List

You may want to have the following supplies available for the activities and projects.

Scissors

Glue sticks

Construction paper

White paper

Stapler and staples

Crayons, colored pencils, markers

Paper fasteners

Tagboard or file folders

Envelopes of various sizes

Yarn in different colors

Using these maps will also help your students meet other standards. For example, Standard 2 states that students should know and understand the physical and human characteristics of places. When students use the base outline map to make a product map or a landform map, they are developing these understandings.

Since we use maps all the time in daily life, all students will benefit from understanding how to read and use them. And maps are also fun! A few suggestions for using the maps are included on pages 6–10.

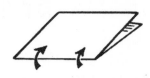

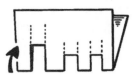

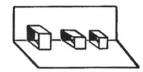

Reports

Students can use the outline maps in a number of ways when they're doing reports about states or countries. Encourage them to use the base outline map as a starting point for creating maps that give a more complete picture of the state or country. They can add symbols to make a produce or resource map, for example. They can include illustrations and photos showing important landforms or tourist sites. Invite them to create their own symbols, or they can use some that are provided in the box on this page. Remind them to include a map key to explain the symbols.

Reports don't have to be flat! Students will be eager to write reports when they are 3-D. Show them how to make pop-up reports by making a pop-up tab (see illustrations and photo).

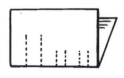

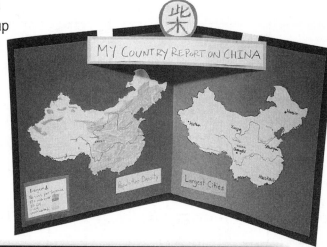

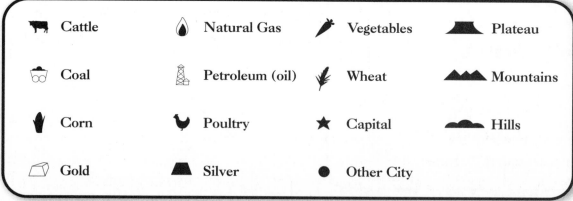

🐄	Cattle	🛢	Natural Gas	🥕	Vegetables	⛰	Plateau
🛒	Coal	⛽	Petroleum (oil)	🌾	Wheat	⛰	Mountains
🌽	Corn	🐔	Poultry	★	Capital	⛰	Hills
◇	Gold	▲	Silver	●	Other City		

Mystery Envelopes

In this activity, students use a series of clues to determine which state or country is being described. Place a copy of a state or country outline map in an 8 1/2- by 11-inch envelope. On the outside of the envelope, write, or have students write, three clues about the state or country. The clues can also be illustrations or photos. Laminating the envelopes will make them sturdier. Punch a hole in the corner of the envelopes and use a metal ring to keep them all together. Students need to read the clues and decide which state or country map is hidden inside.

Scrambled Maps Pictures

The results of this fun activity make a great bulletin-board display. Have copies of the outline maps available to students. Explain that they can use the maps to create pictures. You may wish to use maps of the United States or of all the countries of one continent or region. Have students cut out the maps they want to use and arrange them to make a picture. They should use a state or country only once. When they have finished arranging the maps, have them color in their creations. Suggest that they include an imaginative title or caption. Finally, tell students to make a list of all the states or countries they used in their picture. Hang the finished pictures on a bulletin board. You may want to have on hand the book *The Scrambled States of America* by Laurie Keller.

Map Book

Provide students with several copies of an outline map of either a continent, a country, or a state. Invite them to use the maps to show different things about the continent, country, or state. For example, they can show large cities, or popular tourist destinations, or interesting landforms and bodies of water. They may want to create a personal map that shows places they've visited or would like to visit. Compile all the maps into a class map book.

Map Quilt

Decide on a subject for your quilt. It could be a continent, a hemisphere of the globe, or just a region of the United States. Have each student select a country or a state or states. Explain that they will use the outline map of the country, or state to make a quilt square for a class quilt. Have them color in the map, highlighting important places. Then have them paste each map to a piece of construction paper. Alternate the colors of the background paper. Tape each piece of construction paper together to make a quilt to display on a bulletin board.

Map Mobile

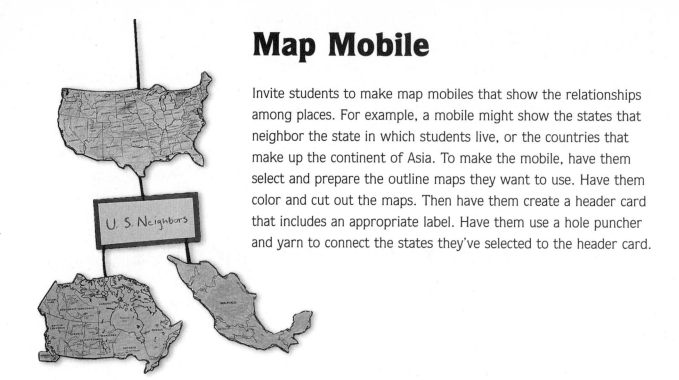

Invite students to make map mobiles that show the relationships among places. For example, a mobile might show the states that neighbor the state in which students live, or the countries that make up the continent of Asia. To make the mobile, have them select and prepare the outline maps they want to use. Have them color and cut out the maps. Then have them create a header card that includes an appropriate label. Have them use a hole puncher and yarn to connect the states they've selected to the header card.

Fan Book

Have students use the state fact sheet on page 9 or the country fact sheet on page 10 to collect information about the state or country they are studying. Then have them color the map. Next, have them paste the map and fact sheet to a piece of tagboard or a file folder. (A legal-size folder works best.) They should paste the map and fact sheet down so the map is above the fact sheet (see photo), and then cut them out as one piece. Have students use these pages to create fan books. You might have them create a fan book for all the states in your region, all the states that neighbor your state, or all the countries of a continent. Attach the pages with a paper fastener and include a first page with a title.

State Facts

After you fill in the blanks, cut out the fact sheet. Follow your teacher's instructions for adding a map at the top.

State _____

Origin of Name _____

Capital _____

Admitted to the Union _____

Motto _____

Song _____

Flower _____

Bird _____

Tree _____

Major Cities _____

_____

Major Rivers _____

_____

Goods and Services _____

_____

_____

Country Facts

After you fill in the blanks, cut out the fact sheet. Follow your teacher's instructions for adding a map at the top.

Country _____

Continent _____

Capital _____

Population_____

Major Languages_____

_____

Major Rivers _____

_____

_____

Largest Cities_____

_____

_____

Goods and Services _____

_____

_____

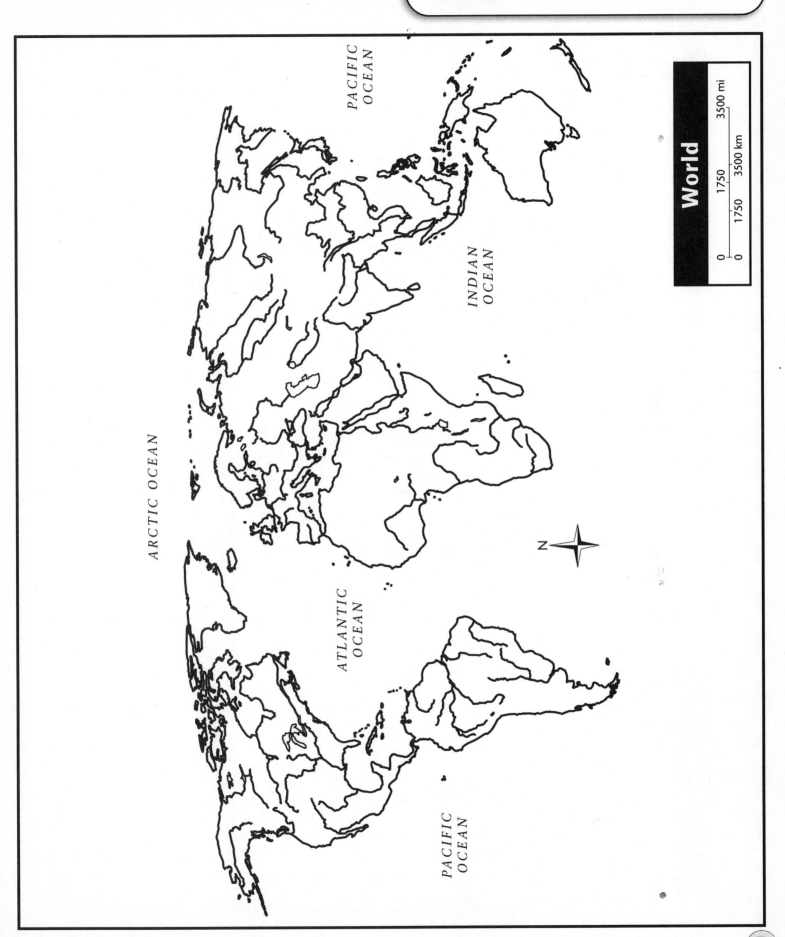

World

3500 mi
1750
3500 km
1750
0
0

PACIFIC
OCEAN

INDIAN
OCEAN

ARCTIC OCEAN

ATLANTIC
OCEAN

PACIFIC
OCEAN

N

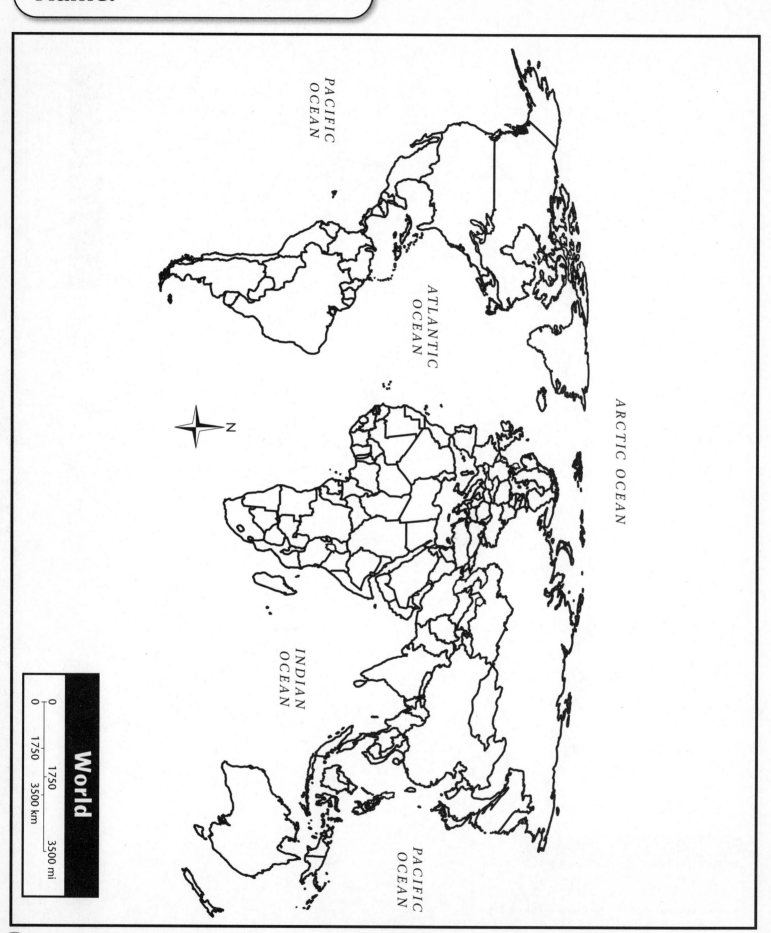

World

0
0
1750
1750
3500 km
3500 mi

PACIFIC OCEAN

ATLANTIC OCEAN

ARCTIC OCEAN

INDIAN OCEAN

PACIFIC OCEAN

N

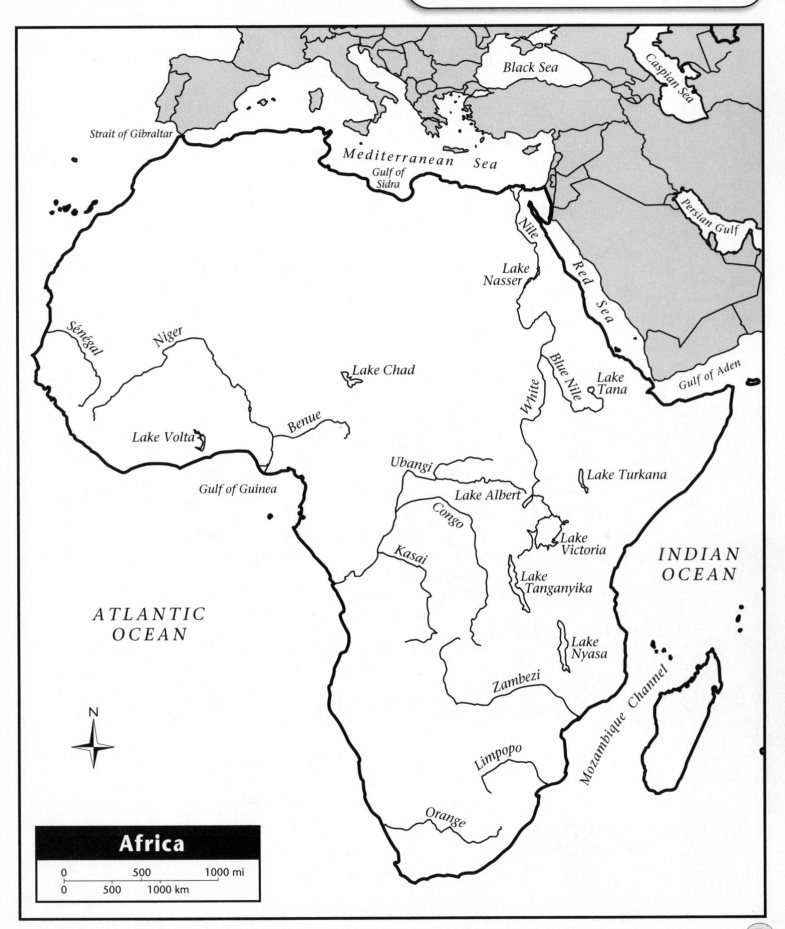

Black Sea

Caspian Sea

Strait of Gibraltar

Mediterranean   Sea

*Gulf of
Sidra*

Persian Gulf

Nile

*Lake
Nasser*

Red   Sea

Sénégal

Niger

Lake Chad

White

Blue Nile

*Lake
Tana*

Gulf of Aden

Benue

Lake Volta

Lake Turkana

Gulf of Guinea

Ubangi

Lake Albert

INDIAN
OCEAN

ATLANTIC
OCEAN

Congo

Kasai

*Lake
Victoria*

*Lake
Tanganyika*

N

*Lake
Nyasa*

Zambezi

Mozambique Channel

Limpopo

Orange

Africa

0	500	1000 mi
0	500	1000 km

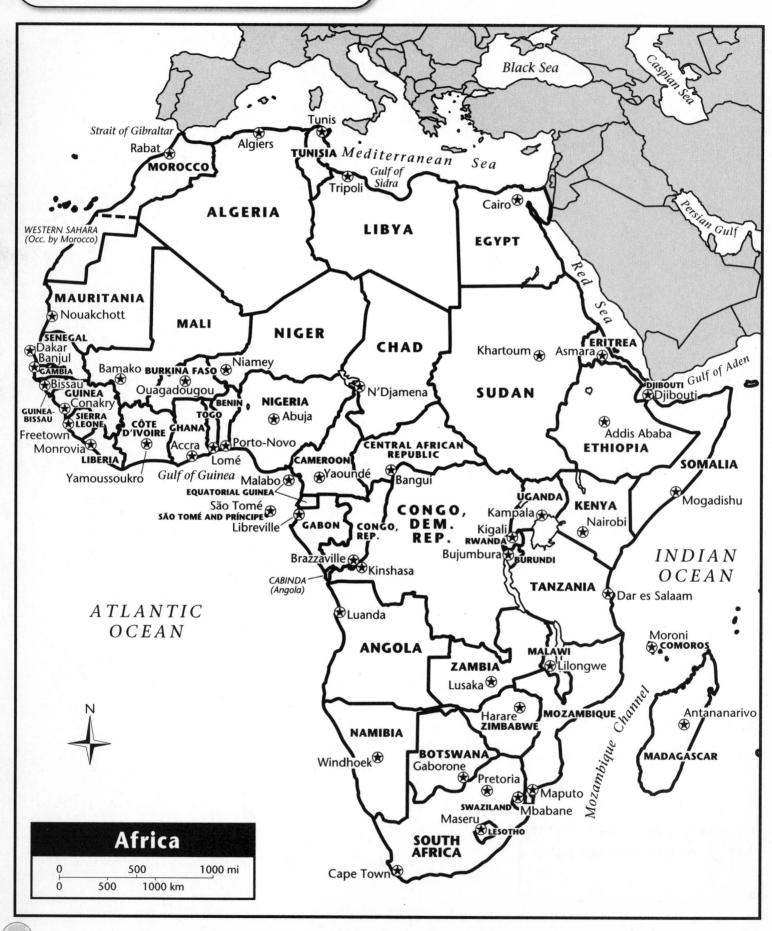

Africa

0   500   1000 mi

0   500   1000 km

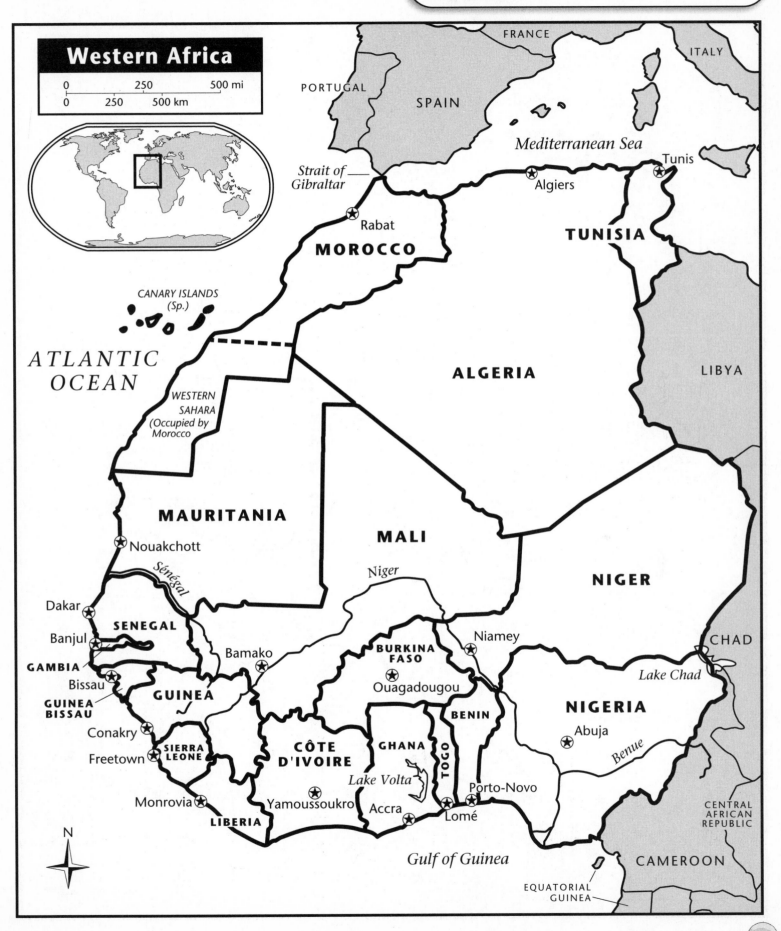

Western Africa

0   250   500 mi
0 250 500 km

PORTUGAL   SPAIN   FRANCE   ITALY

Mediterranean Sea

Strait of ⎯
Gibraltar

Tunis

Algiers

Rabat

MOROCCO   **TUNISIA**

CANARY ISLANDS
(Sp.)

ATLANTIC
OCEAN

ALGERIA   LIBYA

WESTERN
SAHARA
(Occupied by
Morocco)

MAURITANIA

Nouakchott

Sénégal

MALI   *Niger*   **NIGER**

Dakar   **SENEGAL**

Banjul   Bamako

GAMBIA   **BURKINA**   Niamey   CHAD

Bissau   **FASO**   *Lake Chad*

GUINEA   Ouagadougou

GUINEA   **NIGERIA**
BISSAU   **BENIN**

Conakry   Abuja

Freetown   **SIERRA**   **CÔTE**   **GHANA**   *Benue*
LEONE   **D'IVOIRE**   **T**
O
G   Porto-Novo
O
Lake Volta

Monrovia   Yamoussoukro   Accra   Lomé   CENTRAL
AFRICAN
REPUBLIC

LIBERIA

N

Gulf of Guinea   CAMEROON

EQUATORIAL
GUINEA

15

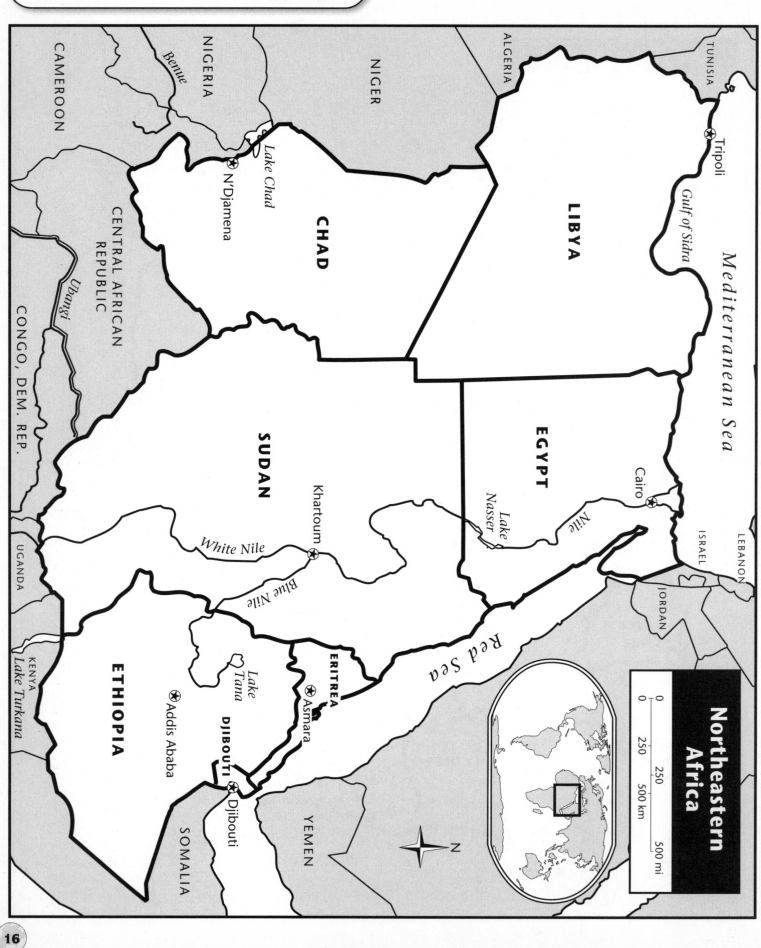

CAMEROON

NIGERIA

Benue

NIGER

ALGERIA

TUNISIA

⊕ Tripoli

Gulf of Sidra

Lake Chad

⊛ N'Djamena

CHAD

LIBYA

Mediterranean Sea

CENTRAL AFRICAN REPUBLIC

Ubangi

CONGO, DEM. REP.

SUDAN

EGYPT

Cairo
⊕

Lake Nasser

Nile

Nile

ISRAEL

LEBANON

JORDAN

Khartoum
⊛

White Nile

Blue Nile

UGANDA

KENYA
Lake Turkana

ETHIOPIA

Lake Tana

⊛ Addis Ababa

ERITREA

⊛ Asmara

DJIBOUTI

⊕ Djibouti

SOMALIA

YEMEN

Red Sea

N

Northeastern Africa

0   250   500 km

0   250   500 mi

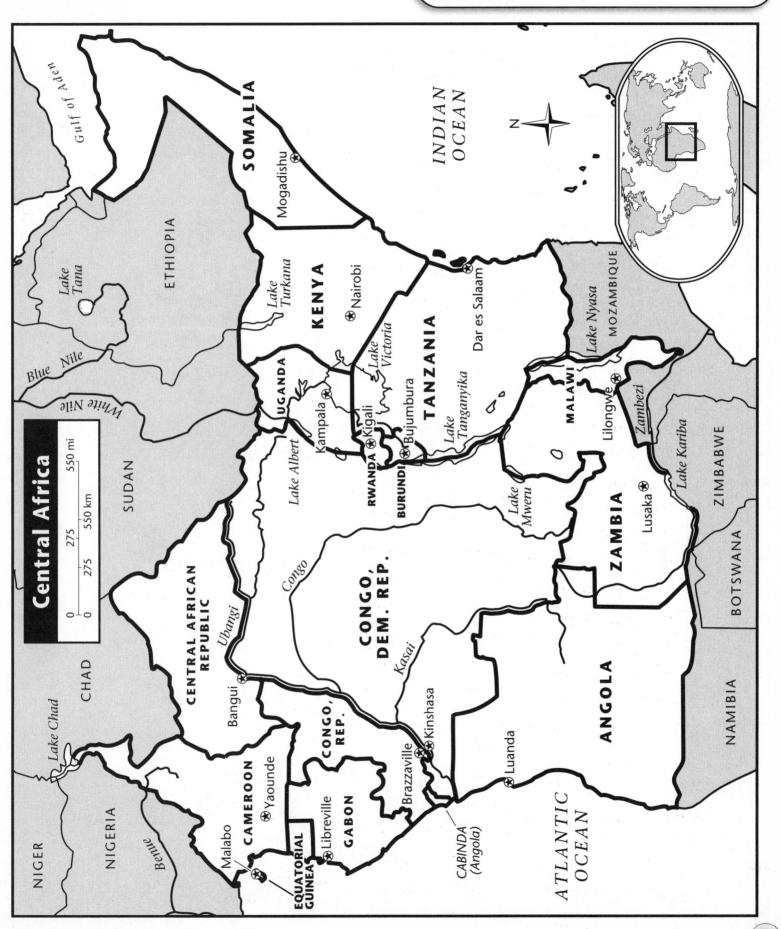

Central Africa

550 mi
275
0

550 km
275
0

Gulf of Aden

SOMALIA

Mogadishu ✶

ETHIOPIA

Lake
Tana

INDIAN
OCEAN

N

Lake
Turkana

KENYA

Nairobi ✶

TANZANIA

Dar es Salaam ✶

Blue Nile

White Nile

SUDAN

UGANDA

Kampala ✶

Lake Albert

Lake
Victoria

RWANDA
Kigali ✶
BURUNDI
Bujumbura ✶

Lake
Tanganyika

MALAWI

Lake Nyasa

MOZAMBIQUE

Lilongwe ✶

Zambezi

Lake Chad

CHAD

CENTRAL AFRICAN
REPUBLIC

Ubangi

Congo

CONGO,
DEM. REP.

Lake
Mweru

ZAMBIA

Lusaka ✶

Lake Kariba

ZIMBABWE

Bangui ✶

Kasai

BOTSWANA

NIGER

NIGERIA

Benue

CAMEROON

Yaounde ✶

CONGO,
REP.

Brazzaville ✶

Kinshasa ✶

Luanda ✶

ANGOLA

NAMIBIA

Malabo

EQUATORIAL
GUINEA

Libreville ✶

GABON

CABINDA
(Angola)

ATLANTIC
OCEAN

17

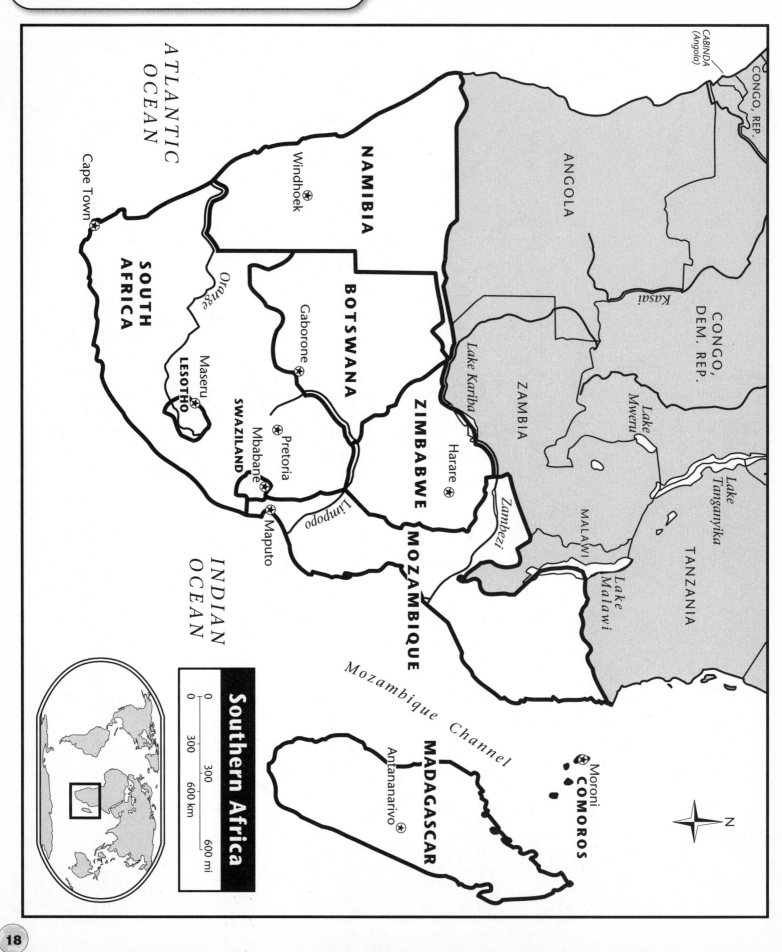

ATLANTIC OCEAN

CABINDA (Angola)

CONGO, REP.

NAMIBIA

ANGOLA

Windhoek ⊛

Cape Town ⊛

SOUTH AFRICA

Orange

BOTSWANA

Gaborone ⊛

Maseru ⊛
LESOTHO

Kasai

CONGO, DEM. REP.

Lake Kariba

ZAMBIA

Lake Mweru

Lake Tanganyika

SWAZILAND
Mbabane ⊛

Pretoria ⊛

ZIMBABWE

Harare ⊛

Zambezi

MALAWI

TANZANIA

Maputo ⊛

Limpopo

MOZAMBIQUE

Lake Malawi

INDIAN OCEAN

Mozambique Channel

Antananarivo ⊛

MADAGASCAR

⊛ Moroni
COMOROS

N

Southern Africa

0	
0	
300	300
600 km	
	600 mi

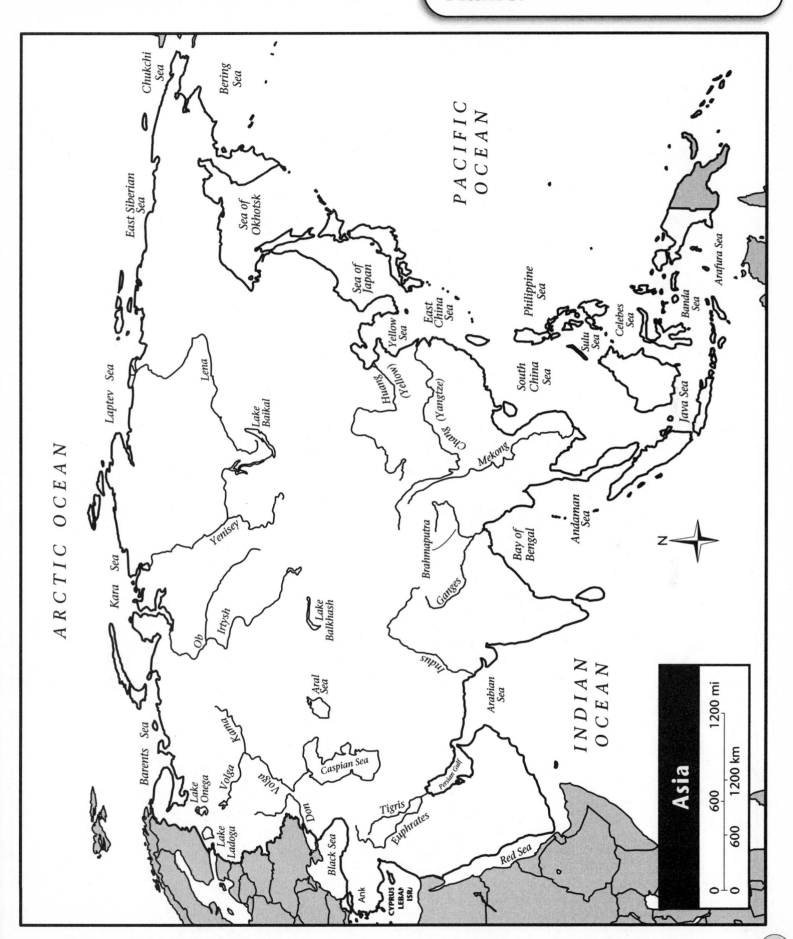

ARCTIC OCEAN

PACIFIC OCEAN

INDIAN OCEAN

Chukchi Sea

Bering Sea

East Siberian Sea

Sea of Okhotsk

Sea of Japan

East China Sea

Philippine Sea

Arafura Sea

Banda Sea

Celebes Sea

Sulu Sea

South China Sea

Yellow (Yellow) Sea

Java Sea

Laptev Sea

Lena

Lake Baikal

Huang (Yellow)

Chang (Yangtze)

Mekong

Andaman Sea

Bay of Bengal

Kara Sea

Yenisey

Ob

Irtysh

Lake Balkhash

Brahmaputra

Ganges

Indus

Arabian Sea

Aral Sea

Arctic Ocean

Barents Sea

Lake Onega

Volga

Kama

Volga

Caspian Sea

Persian Gulf

Lake Ladoga

Don

Tigris

Euphrates

Black Sea

Ank

CYPRUS
LEBAN
ISR/

Red Sea

Asia

0	600	1200 mi
0	600	1200 km

N

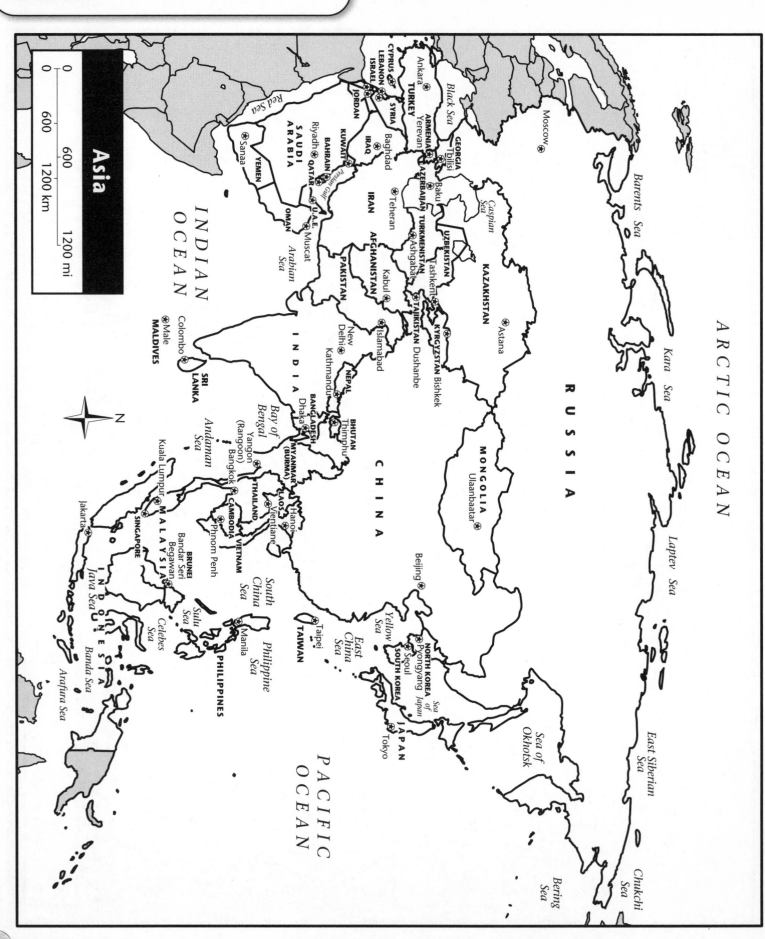

Asia

0
0

600

600

1200 km

1200 mi

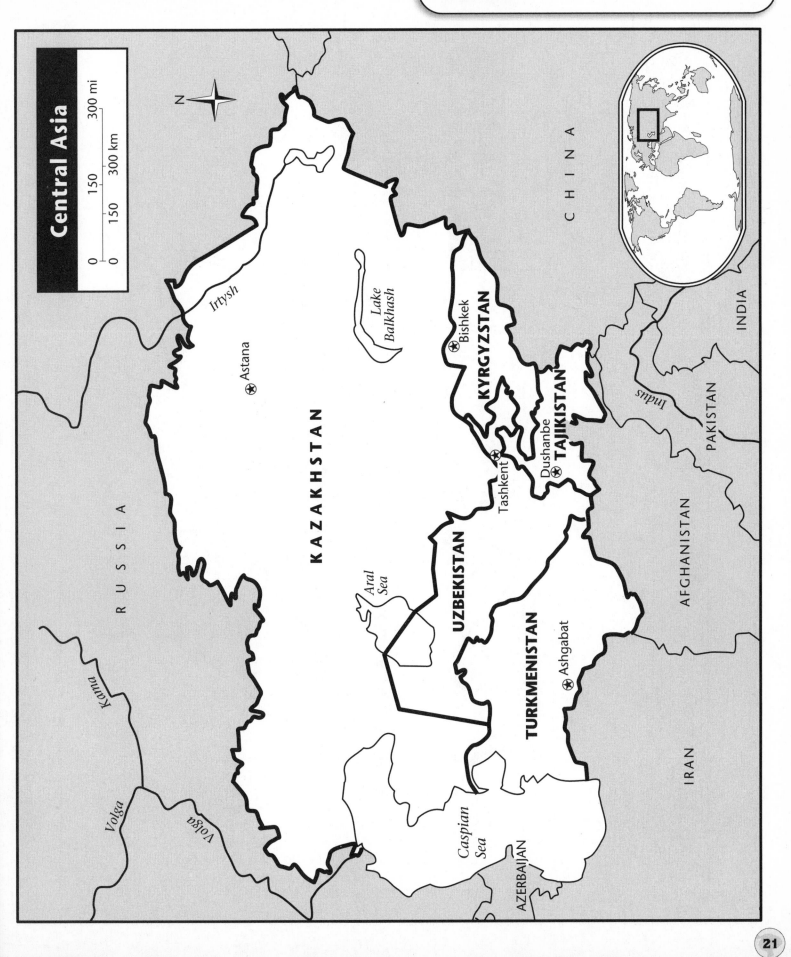

Central Asia

300 mi
300 km
150
150
0
0

N

Irtysh

Lake Balkhash

Bishkek

KYRGYZSTAN

TAJIKISTAN

CHINA

INDIA

Astana

KAZAKHSTAN

Dushanbe

Tashkent

UZBEKISTAN

Indus

PAKISTAN

Aral Sea

AFGHANISTAN

TURKMENISTAN

Ashgabat

RUSSIA

Kama

Volga

Volga

Caspian Sea

AZERBAIJAN

IRAN

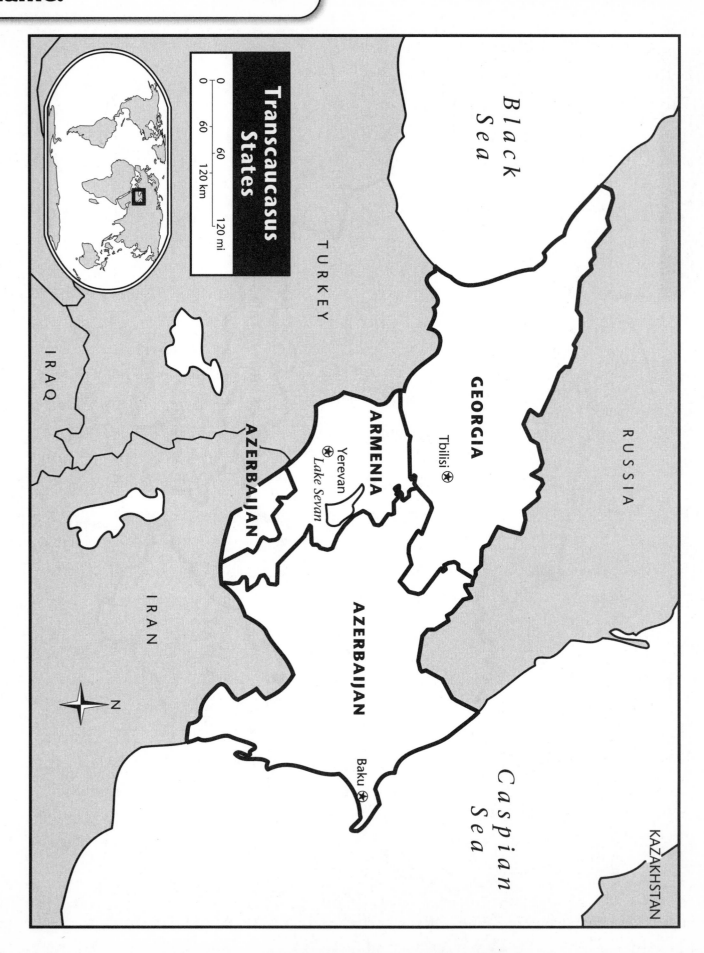

Transcaucasus States

Black Sea

TURKEY

IRAQ

IRAN

GEORGIA

Tbilisi

ARMENIA

Yerevan
Lake Sevan

AZERBAIJAN

AZERBAIJAN

Baku

RUSSIA

Caspian Sea

KAZAKHSTAN

N

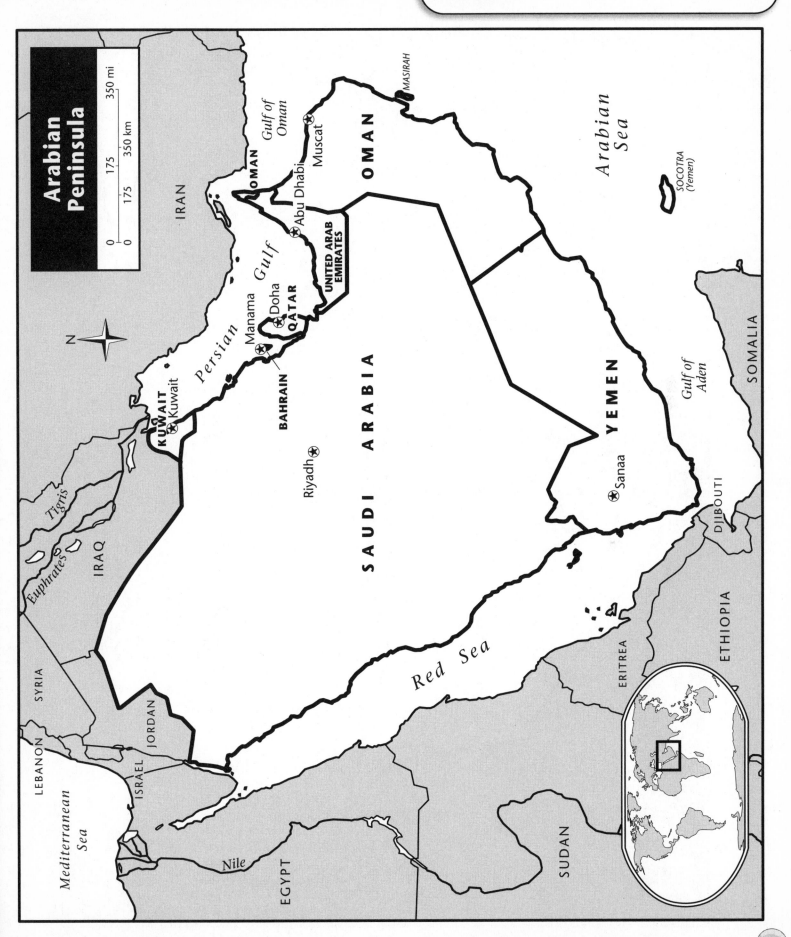

Name:

Arabian Peninsula

350 mi
175
0

350 km
175
0

N

MASIRAH

OMAN

Gulf of
Oman

Muscat

OMAN

Arabian
Sea

SOCOTRA
(Yemen)

IRAN

Abu Dhabi

UNITED ARAB
EMIRATES

Persian

Gulf

Manama

Doha

QATAR

BAHRAIN

Kuwait

KUWAIT

Kuwait

SAUDI ARABIA

Riyadh

YEMEN

Gulf of
Aden

SOMALIA

Sanaa

DJIBOUTI

Tigris

IRAQ

Euphrates

ETHIOPIA

ERITREA

SYRIA

LEBANON

JORDAN

ISRAEL

Red Sea

Mediterranean
Sea

Nile

EGYPT

SUDAN

Name:

EGYPT

BULGARIA

GREECE

GREECE

Mediterranean Sea

Suez Canal

ISRAEL

JORDAN

SAUDI ARABIA

CYPRUS

Nicosia ✪

LEBANON

Beirut ✪

Damascus ✪

SYRIA

IRAQ

Euphrates

Tigris

IRAN

Ankara ✪

Tuz Golu

TURKEY

Black Sea

GEORGIA

ARMENIA

Lake Van

Aras

Turkey, Syria, Lebanon, and Cyprus

0
0
100
100
200 km

100
200 mi

N

24

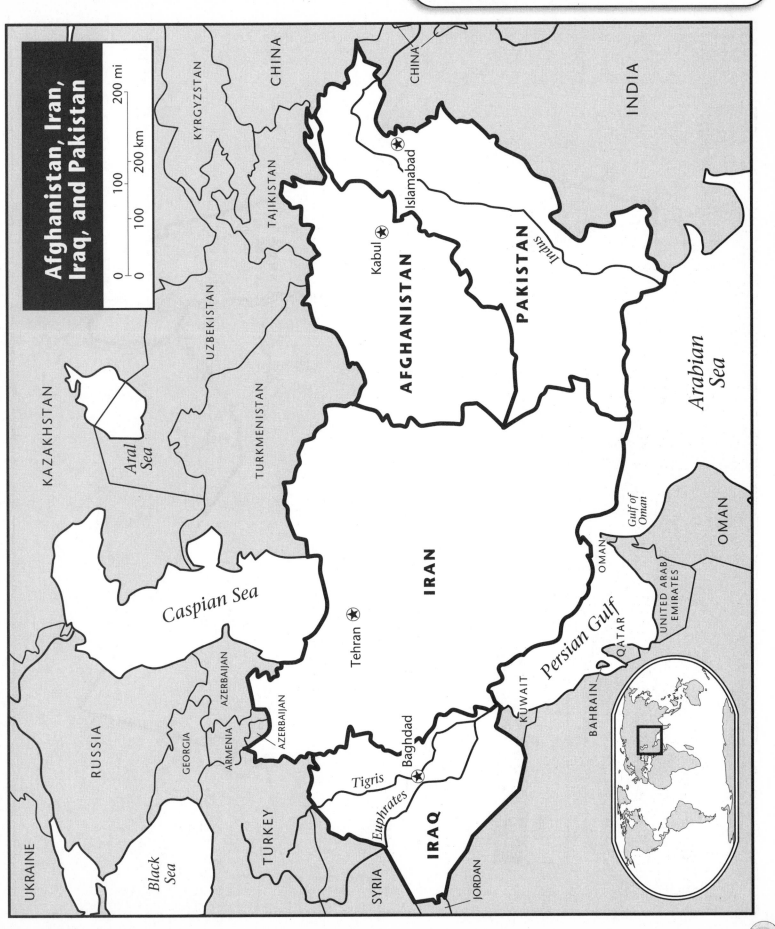

Afghanistan, Iran, Iraq, and Pakistan

200 mi
200 km

CHINA

KYRGYZSTAN

CHINA

INDIA

TAJIKISTAN

Islamabad

Kabul

AFGHANISTAN

PAKISTAN

Indus

UZBEKISTAN

KAZAKHSTAN

Aral Sea

TURKMENISTAN

Arabian Sea

Gulf of Oman

OMAN

Caspian Sea

IRAN

OMAN

UNITED ARAB EMIRATES

AZERBAIJAN

Tehran

Persian Gulf

QATAR

KUWAIT

BAHRAIN

RUSSIA

GEORGIA

ARMENIA

AZERBAIJAN

Baghdad

Tigris

Euphrates

IRAQ

UKRAINE

TURKEY

Black Sea

SYRIA

JORDAN

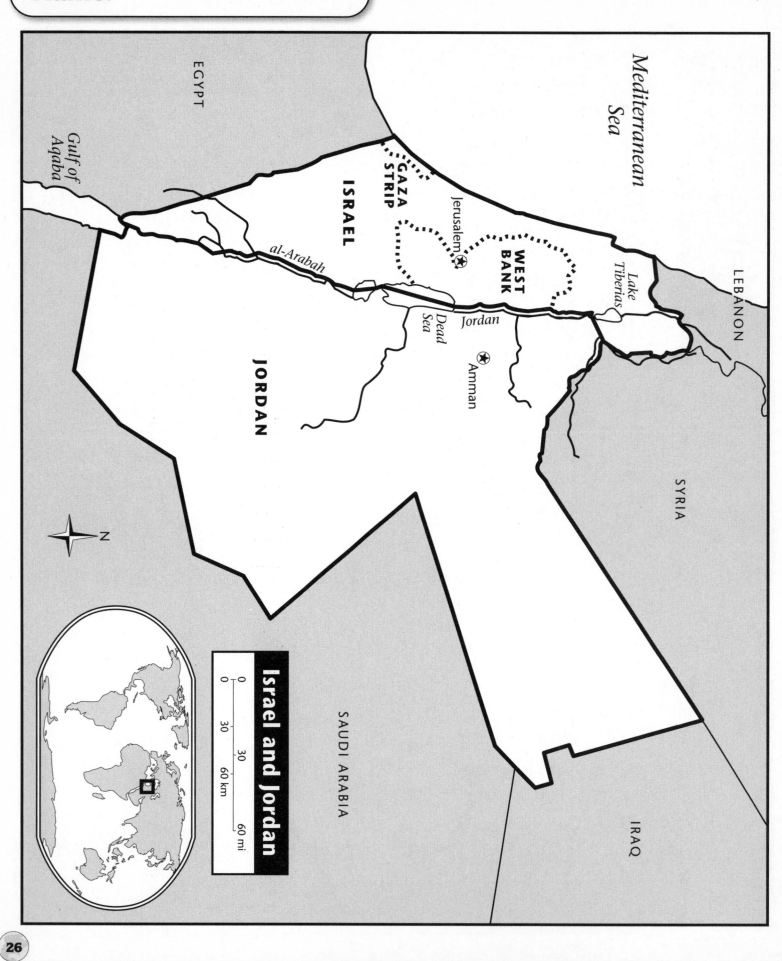

EGYPT

*Mediterranean
Sea*

*Gulf of
Aqaba*

LEBANON

ISRAEL

GAZA
STRIP

Jerusalem

WEST
BANK

Lake
Tiberias

al-Arabah

Dead
Sea

Jordan

SYRIA

JORDAN

Amman

SAUDI ARABIA

IRAQ

N

Israel and Jordan

0   30   60 km

0   30   60 mi

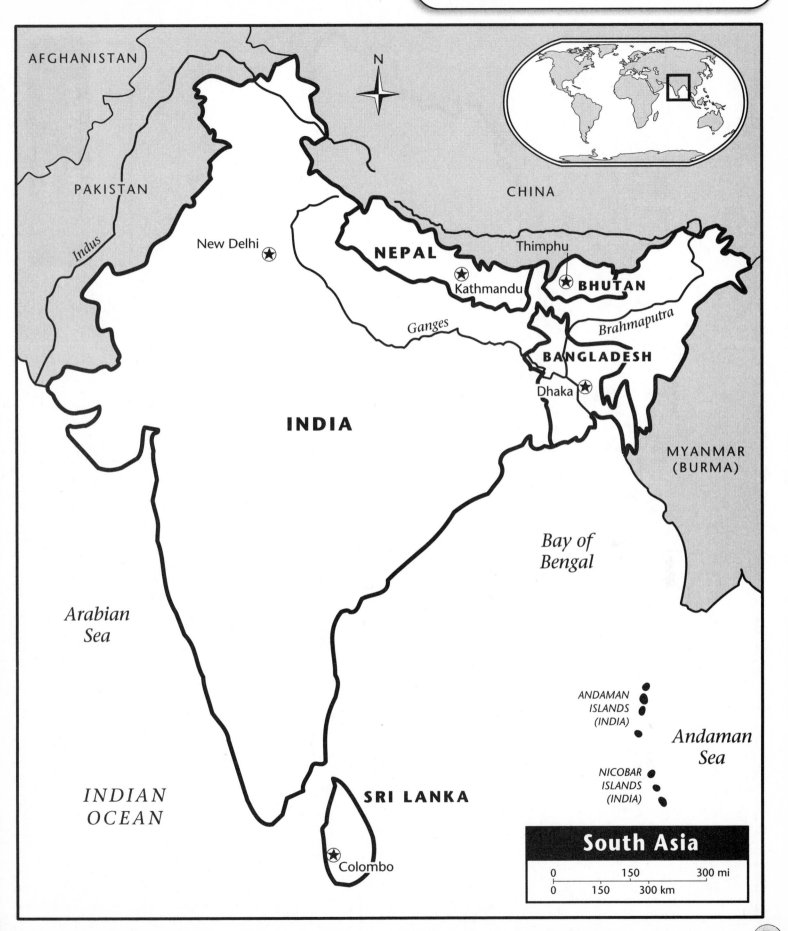

AFGHANISTAN

PAKISTAN

CHINA

Indus

New Delhi ✪

NEPAL

Thimphu

✪
Kathmandu

✪ **BHUTAN**

Ganges

Brahmaputra

BANGLADESH

Dhaka ✪

INDIA

MYANMAR
(BURMA)

*Bay of
Bengal*

*Arabian
Sea*

*Andaman
Sea*

*ANDAMAN
ISLANDS
(INDIA)*

*INDIAN
OCEAN*

SRI LANKA

*NICOBAR
ISLANDS
(INDIA)*

✪ Colombo

N

South Asia

0		150		300 mi
0	150	300 km		

27

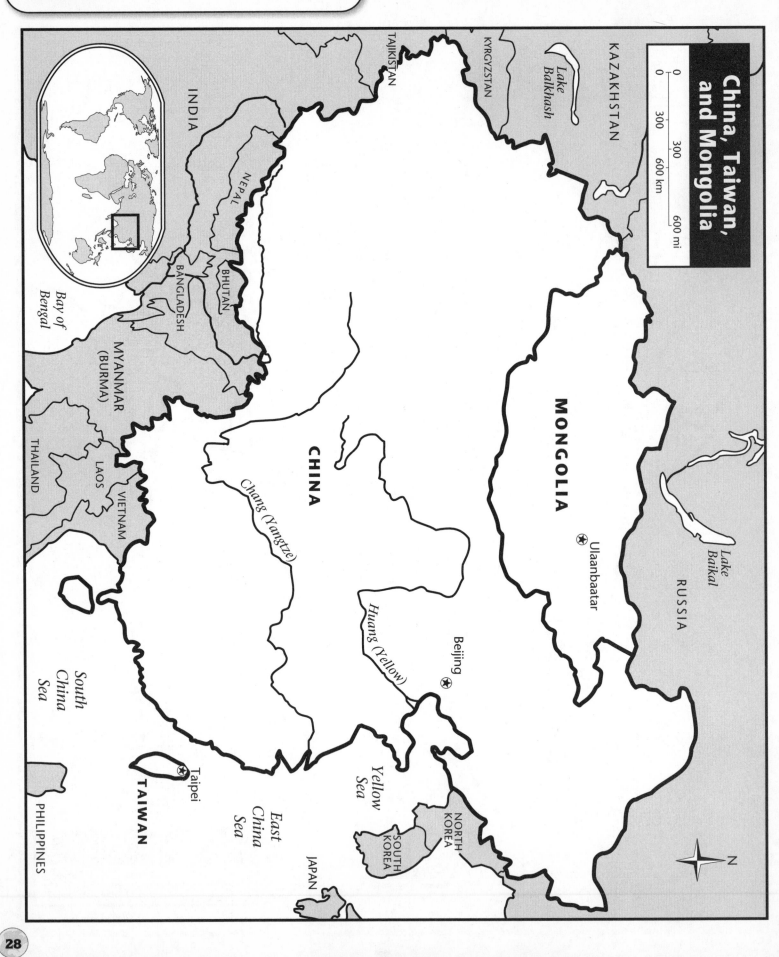

China, Taiwan, and Mongolia

0
0
300
300
600 km
600 mi

KAZAKHSTAN

Lake Balkhash

TAJIKISTAN

KYRGYZSTAN

INDIA

NEPAL

BHUTAN

BANGLADESH

Bay of Bengal

MYANMAR (BURMA)

THAILAND

LAOS

VIETNAM

CHINA

Chang (Yangtze)

MONGOLIA

Ulaanbaatar

Lake Baikal

RUSSIA

Huang (Yellow)

Beijing

South China Sea

Taipei

TAIWAN

Yellow Sea

East China Sea

JAPAN

SOUTH KOREA

NORTH KOREA

PHILIPPINES

N

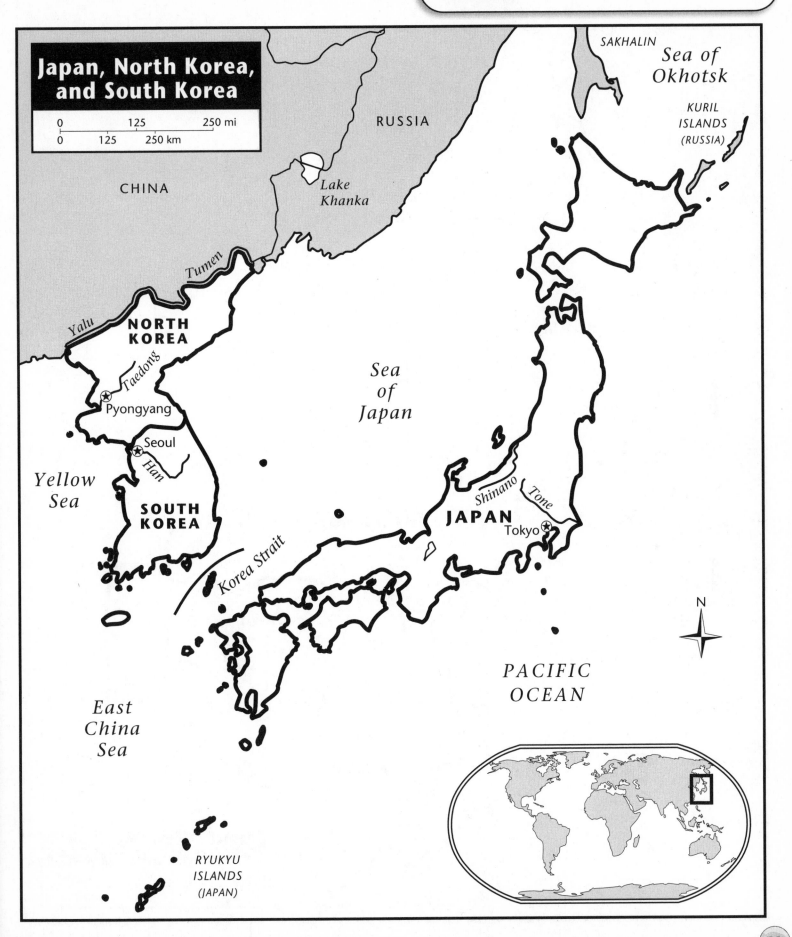

Japan, North Korea, and South Korea

0   125   250 mi
0   125   250 km

CHINA

RUSSIA

Lake Khanka

SAKHALIN

Sea of Okhotsk

KURIL ISLANDS (RUSSIA)

Tumen

Yalu

NORTH KOREA

Taedong

Pyongyang

Seoul

Han

SOUTH KOREA

Yellow Sea

Sea of Japan

Shinano

Tone

JAPAN

Tokyo

Korea Strait

East China Sea

PACIFIC OCEAN

N

RYUKYU ISLANDS (JAPAN)

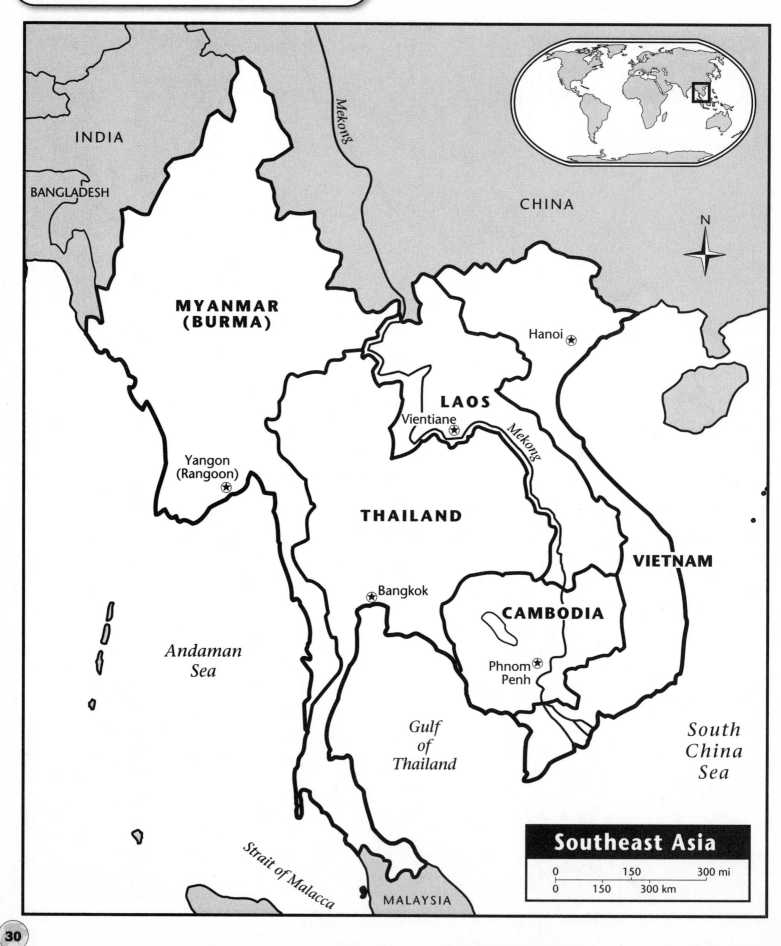

INDIA

BANGLADESH

Mekong

CHINA

N

MYANMAR
(BURMA)

Hanoi ⊛

LAOS

Vientiane ⊛

Mekong

Yangon
(Rangoon) ⊛

THAILAND

VIETNAM

Bangkok ⊛

CAMBODIA

Andaman
Sea

Phnom ⊛
Penh

Gulf
of
Thailand

South
China
Sea

Southeast Asia

| 0 | 150 | 300 mi |

| 0 | 150 | 300 km |

Strait of Malacca

MALAYSIA

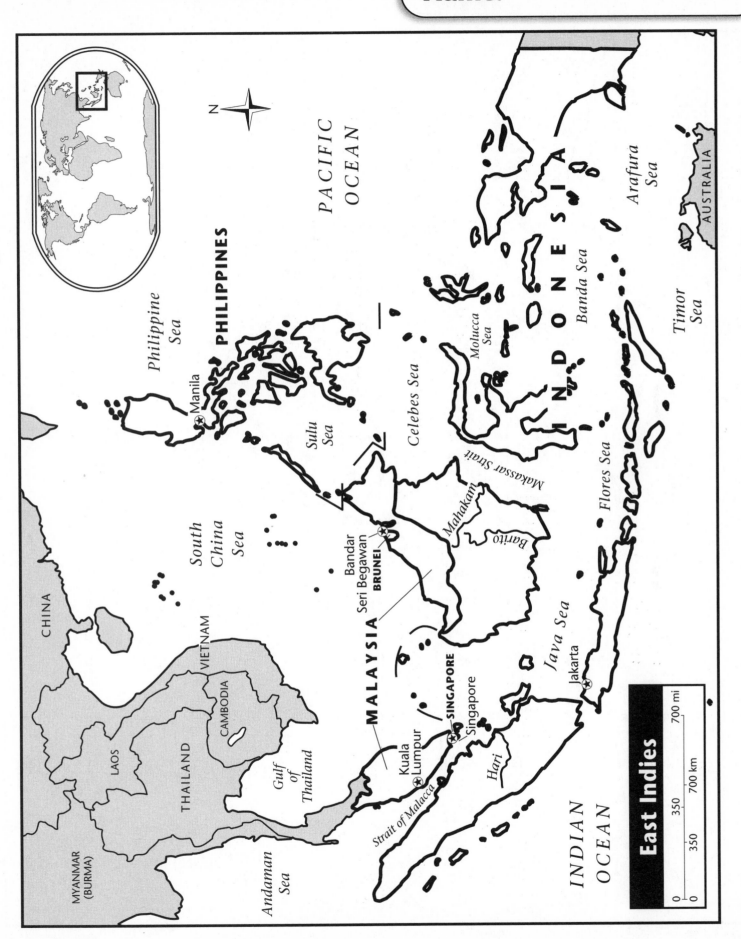

N

PACIFIC
OCEAN

INDONESIA

AUSTRALIA

Arafura
Sea

Banda Sea

PHILIPPINES

Philippine
Sea

Molucca
Sea

Timor
Sea

Manila

Sulu
Sea

Celebes Sea

Makassar Strait

Mahakam

Flores Sea

CHINA

South
China
Sea

Bandar
Seri Begawan

BRUNEI

Barito

Java Sea

Jakarta

VIETNAM

MALAYSIA

SINGAPORE

Singapore

CAMBODIA

LAOS

THAILAND

Gulf
of
Thailand

Kuala
Lumpur

Hari

MYANMAR
(BURMA)

Andaman
Sea

Strait of Malacca

INDIAN
OCEAN

	350		700 mi
0			
0	350		700 km

East Indies

Name:

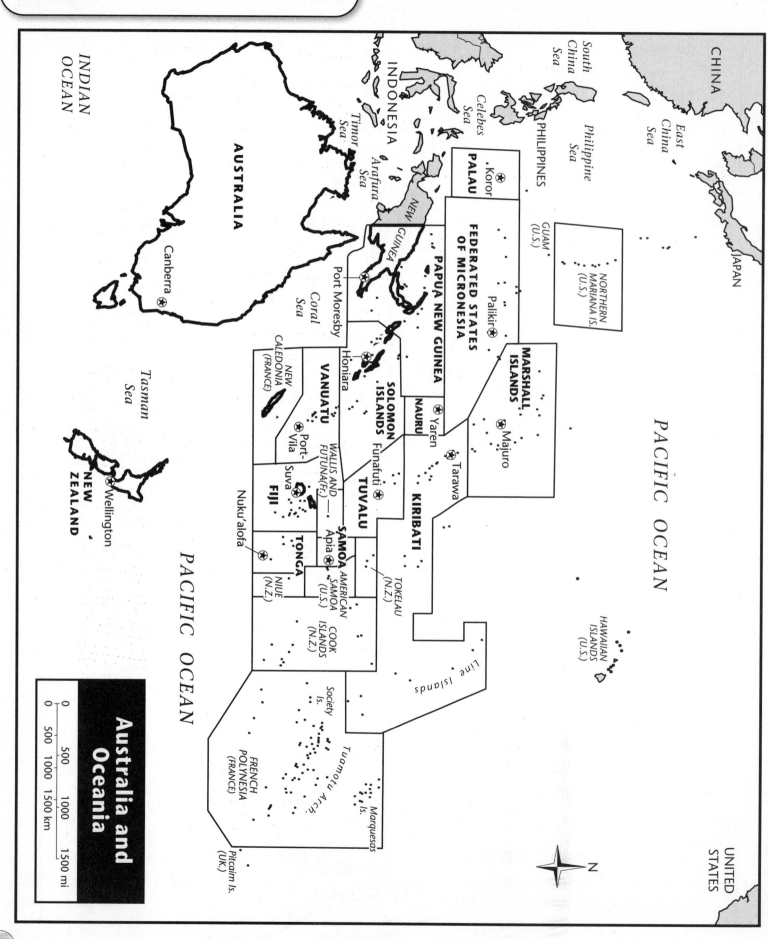

INDIAN OCEAN

South China Sea

East China Sea

CHINA

INDONESIA

Celebes Sea

Philippine Sea

PHILIPPINES

JAPAN

AUSTRALIA

Timor Sea

Arafura Sea

NEW GUINEA

PALAU

• Koror

GUAM (U.S.)

NORTHERN MARIANA IS. (U.S.)

Canberra

FEDERATED STATES OF MICRONESIA

Palikir⊛

PAPUA NEW GUINEA

Port Moresby⊛

Coral Sea

MARSHALL ISLANDS

Majuro⊛

Tasman Sea

NEW CALEDONIA (FRANCE)

VANUATU

Honiara

SOLOMON ISLANDS

NAURU

Yaren⊛

Port-Vila⊛

Funafuti

Tarawa⊛

NEW ZEALAND

Wellington⊛

WALLIS AND FUTUNA(Fr.)

Suva

FIJI

TUVALU

KIRIBATI

Nuku'alofa

TONGA

SAMOA

Apia⊛

AMERICAN SAMOA (U.S.)

TOKELAU (N.Z.)

PACIFIC OCEAN

NIUE (N.Z.)

COOK ISLANDS (N.Z.)

HAWAIIAN ISLANDS (U.S.)

Line Islands

PACIFIC OCEAN

Society Is.

Tuamotu Arch.

Marquesas Is.

FRENCH POLYNESIA (FRANCE)

Pitcairn Is. (U.K.)

N

UNITED STATES

0 500 1000 1500 km
0 500 1000 1500 mi

Australia and Oceania

Pacific Islands

600 mi
600 km
300
300
0
0

N

PACIFIC OCEAN

KIRIBATI

WALLIS AND FUTUNA (FRANCE)

Funafuti

TUVALU

FIJI

PACIFIC

Majuro

Ratik Chain

MARSHALL ISLANDS

Ralik Chain

NAURU

Yaren

SOLOMON ISLANDS

Santa Cruz Islands

VANUATU

Palikir

NORTHERN MARIANA IS. (U.S.)

GUAM (U.S.)

Caroline Islands

FEDERATED STATES OF MICRONESIA

PAPUA NEW GUINEA

Honiara

Guadalcanal

Bismarck Archipelago

NEW GUINEA

Port Moresby

Coral Sea

INDONESIA

AUSTRALIA

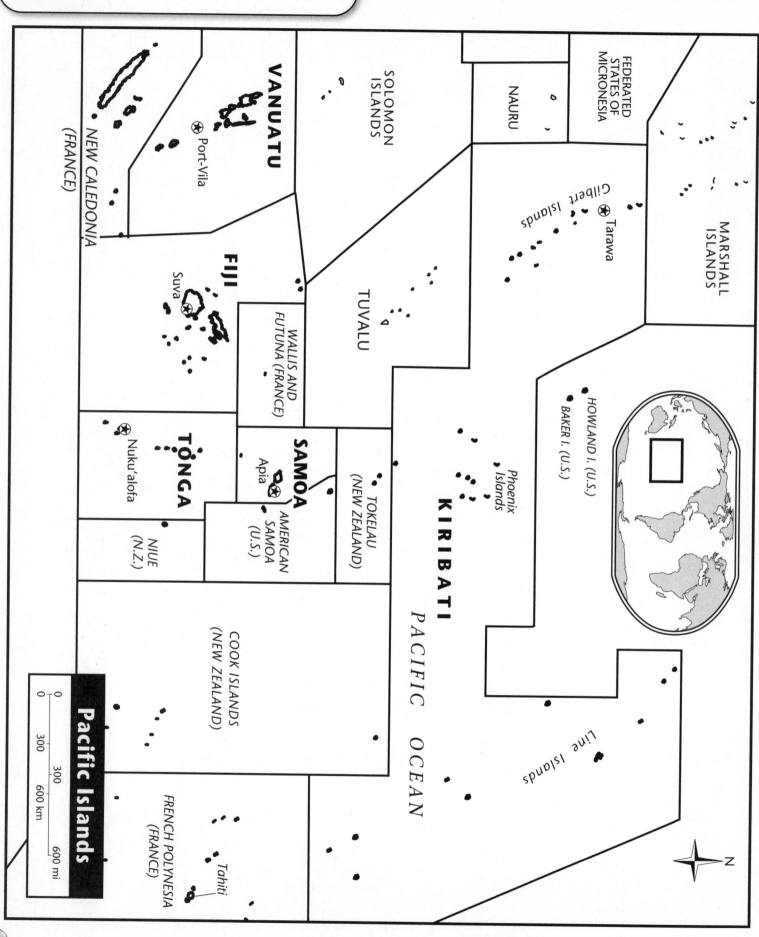

VANUATU

NEW CALEDONIA
(FRANCE)

⊛ Port-Vila

SOLOMON
ISLANDS

NAURU

FEDERATED
STATES OF
MICRONESIA

Gilbert Islands

⊛ Tarawa

MARSHALL
ISLANDS

FIJI

Suva

TUVALU

WALLIS AND
FUTUNA (FRANCE)

TONGA

Nuku'alofa

SAMOA

Apia

AMERICAN
SAMOA
(U.S.)

TOKELAU
(NEW ZEALAND)

Phoenix
Islands

HOWLAND I. (U.S.)

BAKER I. (U.S.)

KIRIBATI

PACIFIC OCEAN

NIUE
(N.Z.)

COOK ISLANDS
(NEW ZEALAND)

Line Islands

FRENCH POLYNESIA
(FRANCE)

Tahiti

N

Pacific Islands

0
0
300
300
600 km
600
mi

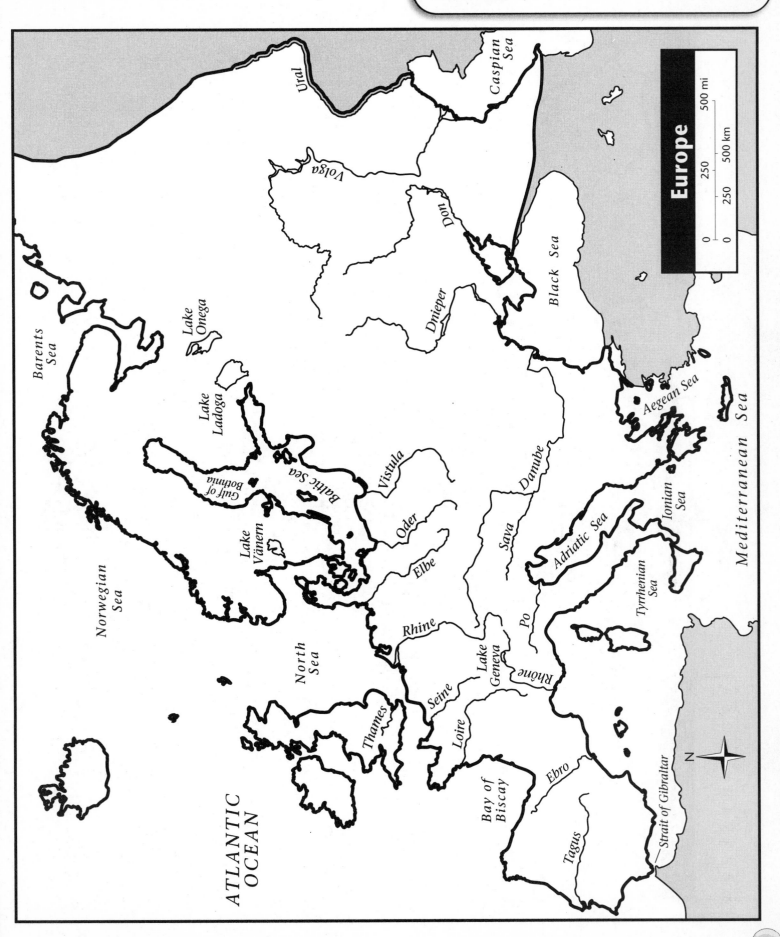

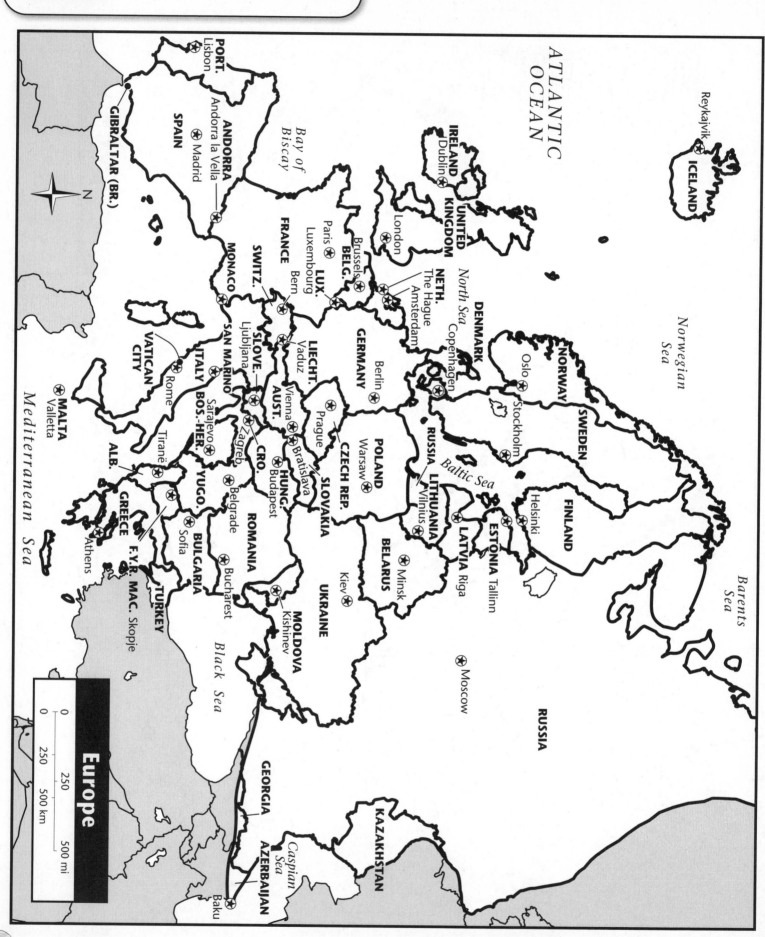

ATLANTIC
OCEAN

Reykajvik
ICELAND

PORT.
Lisbon

GIBRALTAR (BR.)

SPAIN
⊛ Madrid

ANDORRA
⊛ Andorra la Vella

N

IRELAND
Dublin

UNITED
KINGDOM

London

Bay of
Biscay

FRANCE
Paris ⊛
Luxembourg
Bern

LUX.
BELG.
Brussels

MONACO
SWITZ.

NETH.
The Hague
Amsterdam

North Sea

DENMARK
Copenhagen

Norwegian
Sea

Barents
Sea

SAN MARINO
Ljubljana

VATICAN
CITY

SLOVE.
LIECHT.
Vaduz

GERMANY
Berlin

Oslo

NORWAY

SWEDEN

Stockholm

ITALY
Rome

BOS.-HER.
Sarajevo

AUST.
Vienna

Prague

Warsaw

Budapest

CZECH REP.

POLAND

RUSSIA

Baltic Sea

LITHUANIA
Vilnius

Helsinki

FINLAND

MALTA
Valletta

ALB.

Zagreb

CRO.
HUNG.

SLOVAKIA
Bratislava

BELARUS

LATVIA
Riga

ESTONIA
Tallinn

GREECE

Tiranë

YUGO.
Belgrade

ROMANIA

Minsk

Athens

F.Y.R.
MAC. Skopje

BULGARIA
Sofia

Bucharest

UKRAINE
Kiev

Moscow

TURKEY

Black
Sea

MOLDOVA
Kishinev

RUSSIA

Mediterranean Sea

GEORGIA

KAZAKHSTAN

Caspian
Sea

AZERBAIJAN
Baku

Europe

0
0
250
250
500 km
500 mi

United Kingdom and Ireland

0   100   200 mi
0   100   200 km

SHETLAND ISLANDS

ORKNEY ISLANDS

SCOTLAND

N

North Sea

NORTHERN IRELAND

ISLE OF MAN (U.K.)

Dublin

Irish Sea

IRELAND

UNITED KINGDOM

ENGLAND

WALES

Celtic Sea

London

ATLANTIC OCEAN

ISLE OF WIGHT

English Channel

BELGIUM

CHANNEL ISLANDS

FRANCE

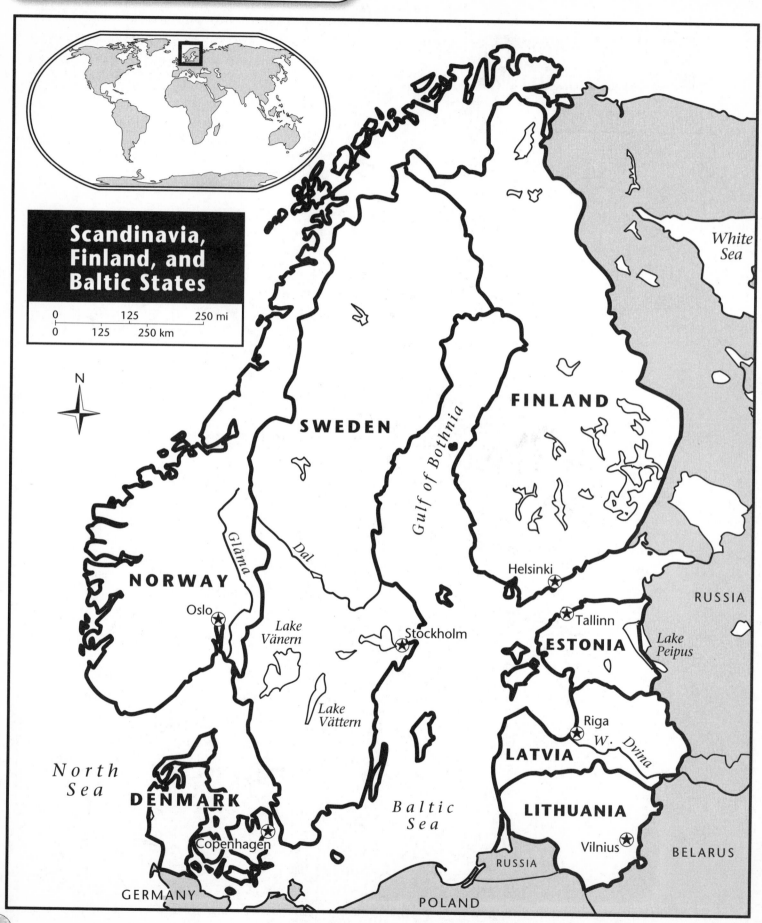

Scandinavia, Finland, and Baltic States

0   125   250 mi
0   125   250 km

N

White Sea

FINLAND

SWEDEN

Gulf of Bothnia

NORWAY

Glåma

Dal

Oslo

Lake Vänern

Stockholm

Lake Vättern

Helsinki

Tallinn

ESTONIA

Lake Peipus

RUSSIA

Riga

W. Dvina

LATVIA

North Sea

DENMARK

Baltic Sea

LITHUANIA

Vilnius

BELARUS

Copenhagen

RUSSIA

GERMANY

POLAND

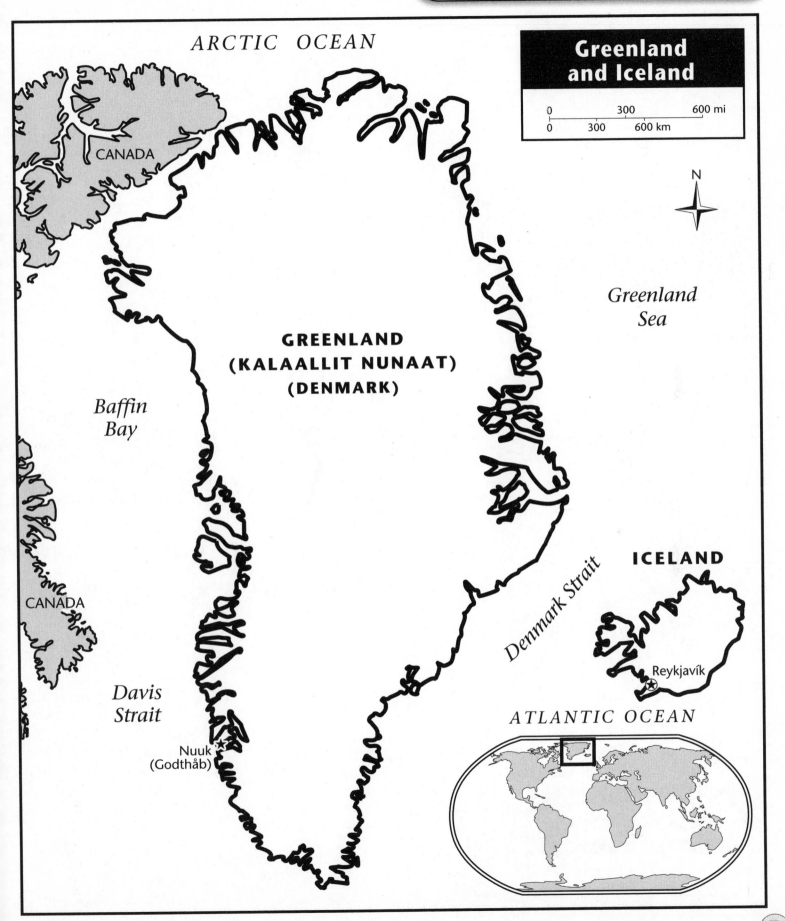

ARCTIC OCEAN

Greenland
and Iceland

0   300   600 mi
0   300   600 km

N

CANADA

Greenland
Sea

GREENLAND
(KALAALLIT NUNAAT)
(DENMARK)

Baffin
Bay

CANADA

ICELAND

Denmark Strait

Reykjavík

Davis
Strait

ATLANTIC OCEAN

Nuuk
(Godthåb)

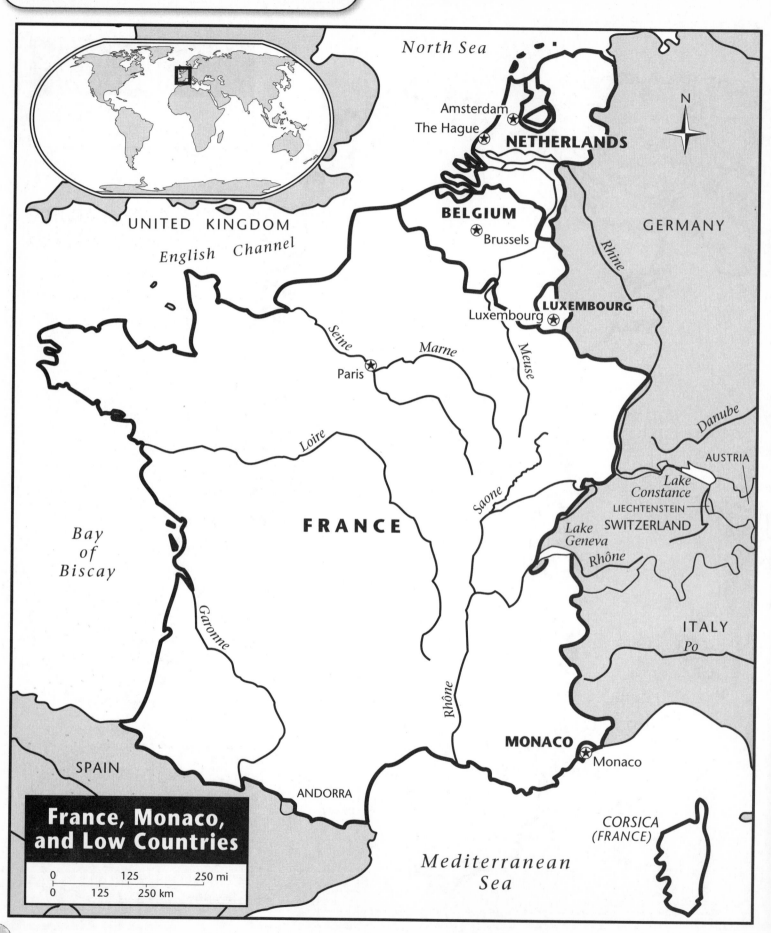

North Sea

Amsterdam
The Hague
NETHERLANDS

BELGIUM
• Brussels

GERMANY

Rhine

UNITED KINGDOM

English Channel

LUXEMBOURG
Luxembourg

Meuse

N

Seine
Marne
Paris

Danube

Loire

AUSTRIA

Saone

Lake Constance

LIECHTENSTEIN
SWITZERLAND

FRANCE

Bay of Biscay

Lake Geneva

Rhône

Garonne

ITALY
Po

Rhône

MONACO
Monaco

SPAIN

ANDORRA

Mediterranean Sea

CORSICA (FRANCE)

France, Monaco, and Low Countries

0	125	250 mi
0	125	250 km

N

North
Sea

DENMARK

*Baltic
Sea*

West Central Europe

0   100   200 mi

0   100   200 km

Elbe

⊛ Berlin

Oder

POLAND

NETHERLANDS

BELGIUM

GERMANY

Rhine

LUXEMBOURG

CZECH
REPUBLIC

SLOVAKIA

FRANCE

Danube

Vienna ⊛

*Lake
Constance*

AUSTRIA

*Lake
Balaton*

Bern ⊛   Vaduz ⊛ **LIECHTENSTEIN**

HUNGARY

*Lake
Geneva*   **SWITZERLAND**

Rhône

ITALY

SLOVENIA

CROATIA

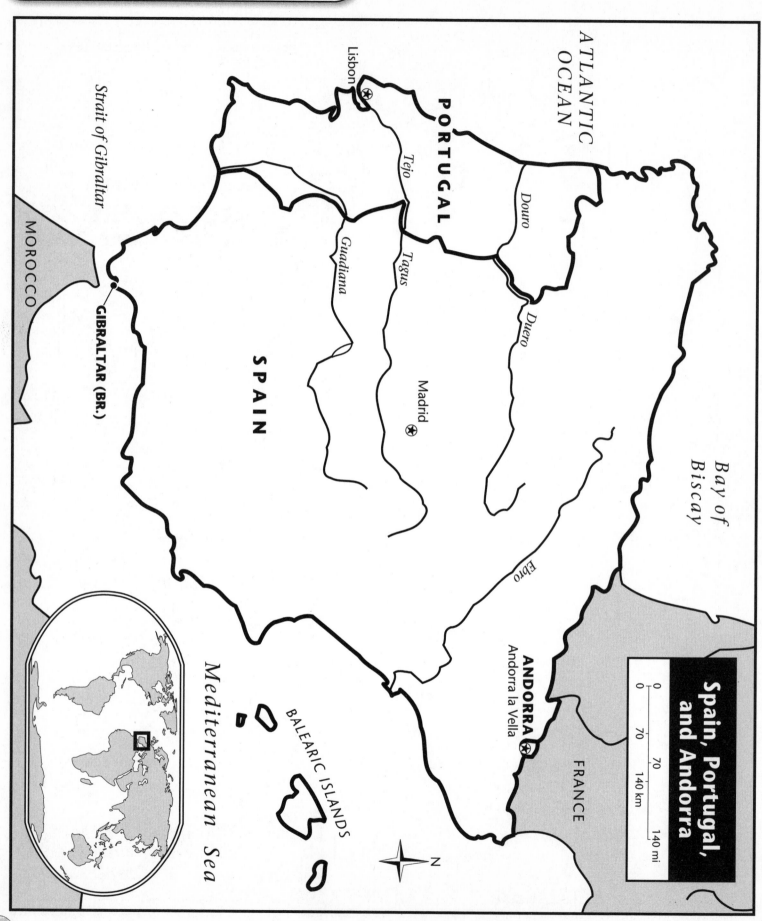

ATLANTIC
OCEAN

Strait of Gibraltar

MOROCCO

GIBRALTAR (BR.)

Lisbon

PORTUGAL

Tejo

Douro

Guadiana

Tagus

Duero

S P A I N

Madrid

Bay of
Biscay

Ebro

ANDORRA
Andorra la Vella

FRANCE

Mediterranean Sea

BALEARIC ISLANDS

N

Spain, Portugal,
and Andorra

0   70   140 km
0   70   140 mi

SWITZERLAND

Rhine

AUSTRIA

HUNGARY

Rhône

Rhône

L. Como

Adige

Lake Maggiore

Ljubljana

Drava

Zagreb

FRANCE

Po

Lake Garda

SLOVENIA

CROATIA

Danube

Po

Gulf of Venice

Sava

BOSNIA AND HERZEGOVINA

Gulf of Genoa

Arno

SAN MARINO

Sarajevo

MONACO

Ligurian Sea

Adriatic Sea

YUGOSLAVIA

ELBA

CORSICA (FRANCE)

ITALY

Tiber

CROATIA

VATICAN CITY Rome

ALBANIA

SARDINIA (ITALY)

Tyrrhenian Sea

CAPRI

Gulf of Taranto

Ionian Sea

Mediterranean Sea

N

SICILY (ITALY)

Southern Europe

0	50	100	150 mi
0	50	100	150 km

Valletta

MALTA

Name:

The Balkan States

0   50   100   150   200 mi
0   50   100   150 200 km

UKRAINE

MOLDOVA

AUSTRIA

Lake Balaton

HUNGARY

Danube

ROMANIA

Prut

CROATIA

Sava

Bucharest ✪ *Danube*

Belgrade

Black Sea

BOSNIA & HERZEGOVINA

YUGOSLAVIA

BULGARIA

✪ Sofia

Adriatic Sea

Skopje ✪

MACEDONIA

Tiranë ✪

ALBANIA

ITALY

Aegean Sea

GREECE

Athens ✪

Ionian Sea

Sea of Crete

RHODES (GREECE)

Mediterranean Sea

CRETE (GREECE)

44

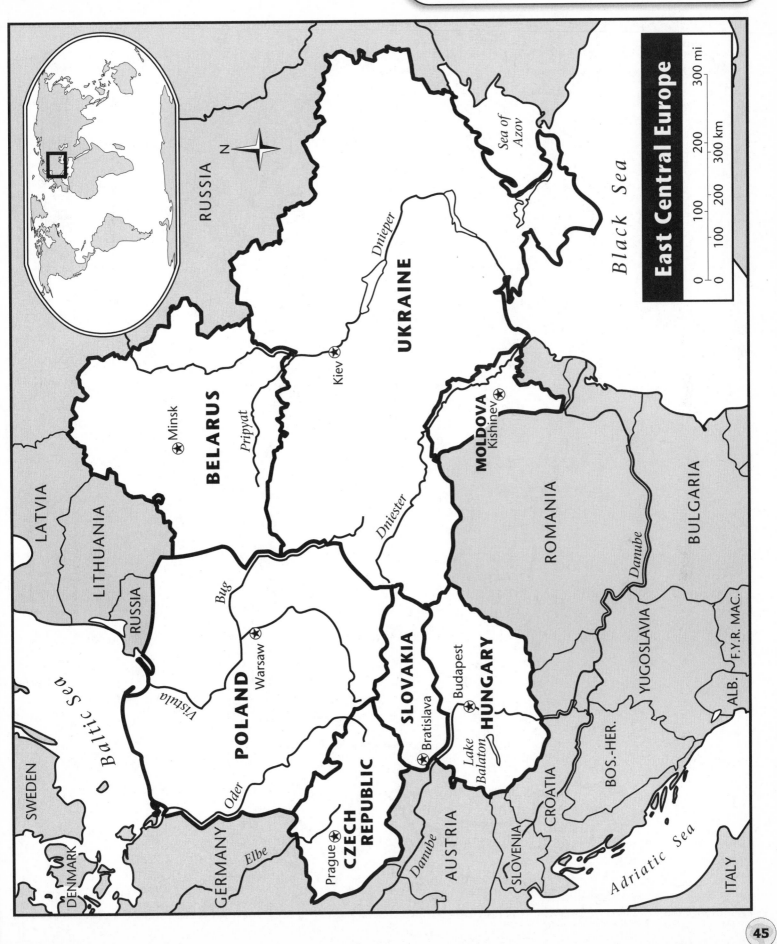

East Central Europe

300 mi

300 km

0   100   200   300

0   100   200   300

RUSSIA

N

Dnieper

UKRAINE

Sea of Azov

Black Sea

Kiev

BELARUS

Minsk

Pripyat

MOLDOVA

Kishinev

Dniester

ROMANIA

BULGARIA

Danube

LATVIA

LITHUANIA

RUSSIA

Bug

Vistula

POLAND

Warsaw

Oder

GERMANY

Elbe

Baltic Sea

SWEDEN

DENMARK

CZECH REPUBLIC

Prague

SLOVAKIA

Bratislava

Lake Balaton

Budapest

HUNGARY

Danube

AUSTRIA

SLOVENIA

CROATIA

BOS.-HER.

YUGOSLAVIA

ALB.

F.Y.R. MAC.

Adriatic Sea

ITALY

45

Name:

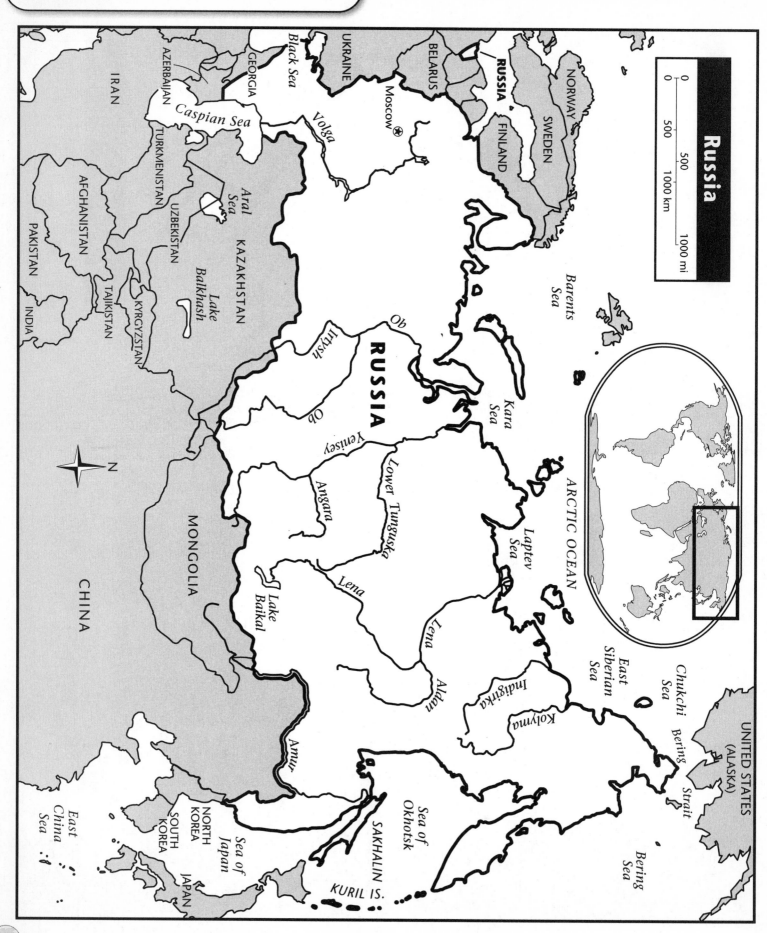

Russia

ARCTIC OCEAN

Bering Strait

Bering Sea

Beaufort Sea

Baffin Bay

Denmark Strait

Davis Strait

Yukon R.

Mackenzie R.

Great Bear Lake

Gulf of Alaska

Great Slave Lake

Lake Athabasca

Labrador Sea

Peace R.

Athabasca R.

Hudson Bay

Fraser R.

Columbia R.

Saskatchewan R.

Lake Winnipeg

James Bay

St. Lawrence R.

Missouri R.

Lake Superior

Snake R.

Lake Michigan

L. Huron

Lake Ontario

Great Salt Lake

L. Erie

PACIFIC OCEAN

Colorado R.

Platte R.

Ohio R.

Arkansas R.

Mississippi R.

ATLANTIC OCEAN

Rio Grande

Gulf of Mexico

Bay of Campeche

Caribbean Sea

North America

0   200   400   600   800 mi

0   400   800 km

Name:

ARCTIC OCEAN

Bering Strait

Bering Sea

ALASKA (U.S)

Beaufort Sea

GREENLAND (DENMARK)

Baffin Bay

Denmark Strait

Davis Strait

Gulf of Alaska

Labrador Sea

Hudson Bay

CANADA

N

Ottawa ✦

UNITED STATES

Washington, D.C. ✦

PACIFIC OCEAN

ATLANTIC OCEAN

BAHAMAS
Nassau ✦

PUERTO RICO (U.S.)

Gulf of Mexico

DOMINICAN REPUBLIC

Havana ✦

CUBA

Santo Domingo ✦

MEXICO

Bay of Campeche

JAMAICA
Kingston ✦

HAITI Port-au-Prince

Mexico City ✦

BELIZE
Belmopan ✦

Caribbean Sea

HONDURAS Tegucigalpa ✦

NICARAGUA

GUATEMALA Guatemala City

✦ Managua

PANAMA Panama City

EL SALVADOR San Salvador

COSTA RICA San José

North America

| 0 | 200 | 400 | 600 | 800 mi |
| 0 | | 400 | | 800 km |

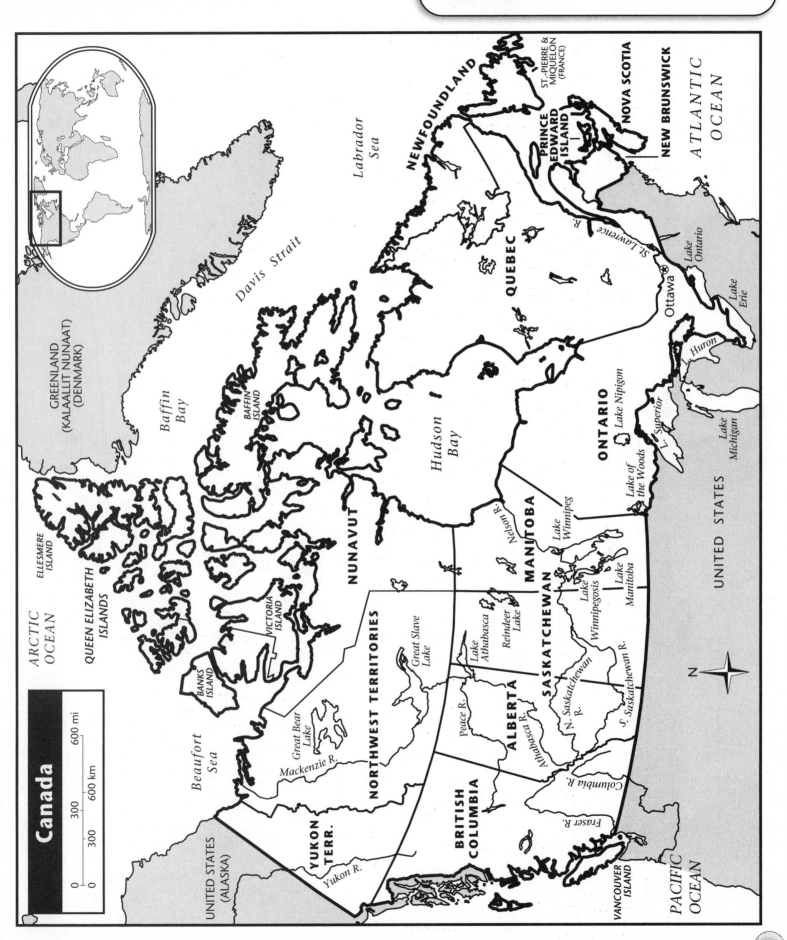

Canada

600 mi
600 km
300
300
0
0

ARCTIC OCEAN

GREENLAND (KALAALLIT NUNAAT) (DENMARK)

ELLESMERE ISLAND

QUEEN ELIZABETH ISLANDS

BANKS ISLAND

VICTORIA ISLAND

BAFFIN ISLAND

Baffin Bay

Davis Strait

Labrador Sea

NEWFOUNDLAND

ST.-PIERRE & MIQUELON (FRANCE)

NOVA SCOTIA

NEW BRUNSWICK

PRINCE EDWARD ISLAND

ATLANTIC OCEAN

St. Lawrence R.

QUEBEC

Hudson Bay

Lake Ontario

Lake Erie

L. Huron

Lake Michigan

L. Superior

Lake Nipigon

ONTARIO

Lake of the Woods

Ottawa

UNITED STATES

NUNAVUT

Beaufort Sea

Great Bear Lake

Mackenzie R.

NORTHWEST TERRITORIES

Great Slave Lake

Lake Athabasca

Reindeer Lake

Lake Winnipeg

Nelson R.

MANITOBA

Lake Winnipegosis

Lake Manitoba

SASKATCHEWAN

N. Saskatchewan R.

S. Saskatchewan R.

Saskatchewan R.

ALBERTA

Athabasca R.

Peace R.

Columbia R.

BRITISH COLUMBIA

Fraser R.

YUKON TERR.

Yukon R.

UNITED STATES (ALASKA)

VANCOUVER ISLAND

PACIFIC OCEAN

N

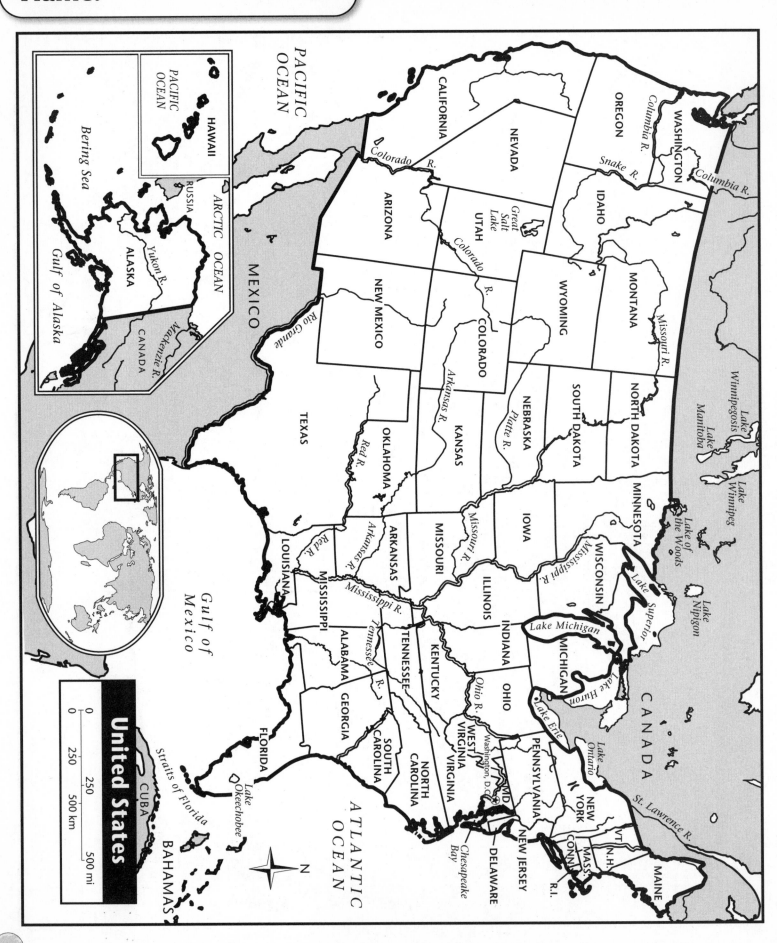

United States

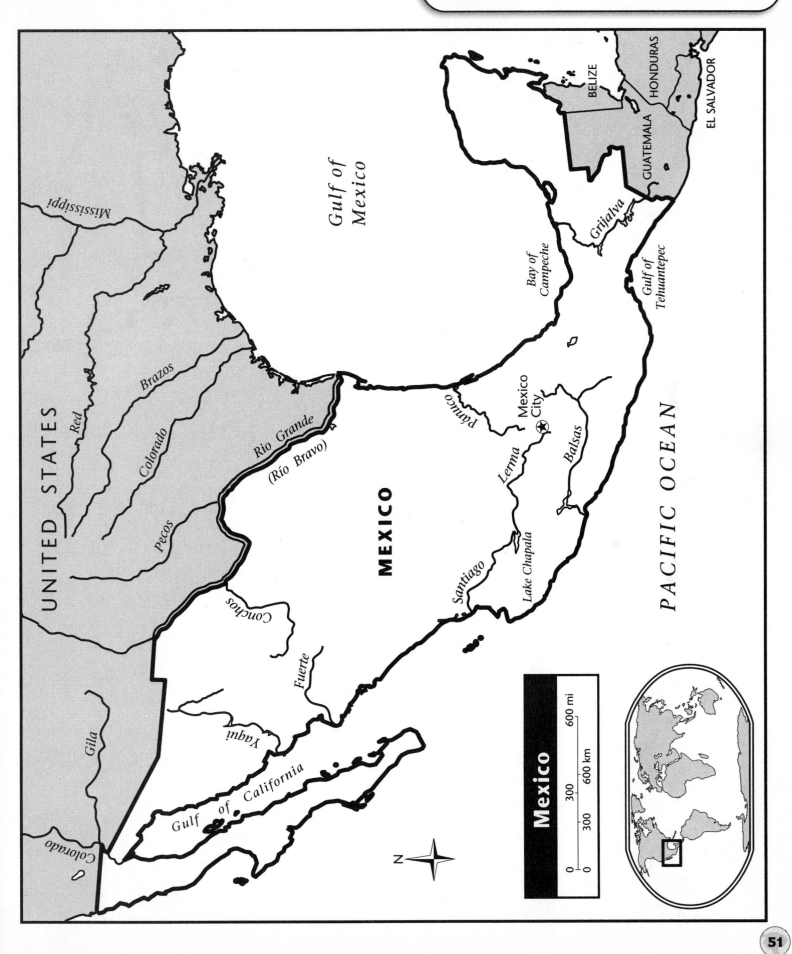

UNITED STATES

Mississippi

Gulf of
Mexico

BELIZE

GUATEMALA

HONDURAS

EL SALVADOR

Grijalva

Bay of
Campeche

Gulf of
Tehuantepec

Red

Brazos

Colorado

Rio Grande

(Río Bravo)

Pecos

Pánuco

Mexico
City

Lerma

Balsas

MEXICO

Santiago

Lake Chapala

PACIFIC OCEAN

Conchos

Fuerte

Gila

Yaqui

Gulf of California

Colorado

N

Mexico

| 600 mi |
| 300 |
| 0 |

| 600 km |
| 300 |
| 0 |

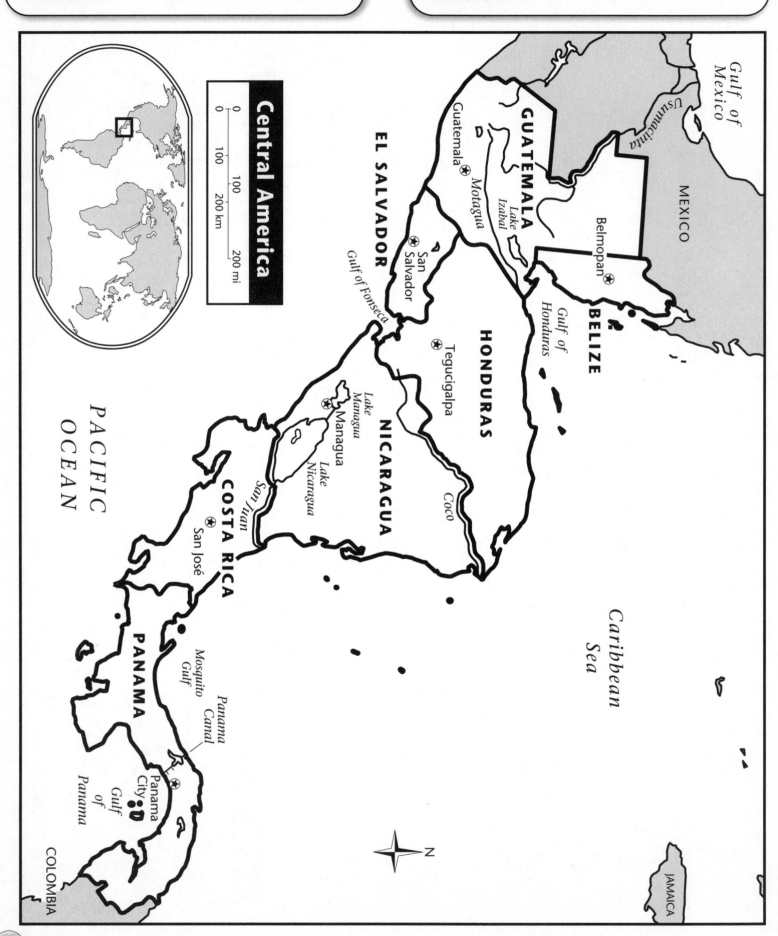

Central America

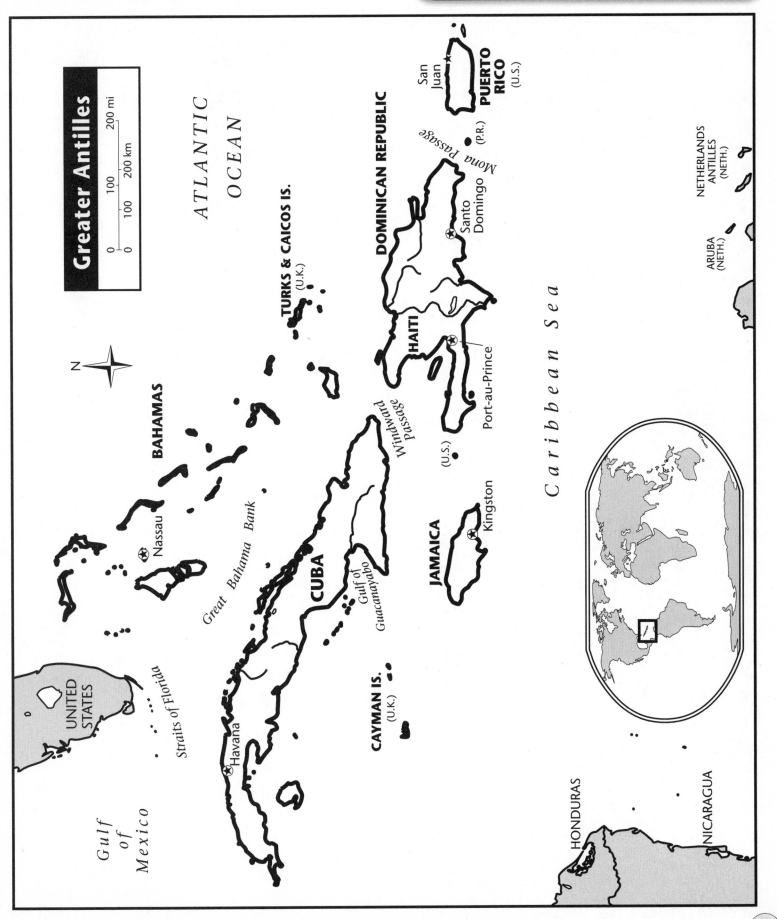

Greater Antilles

200 mi
200 km
0 100 200
0 100 200

ATLANTIC OCEAN

N

BAHAMAS

Nassau

Straits of Florida

Great Bahama Bank

UNITED STATES

Gulf of Mexico

Havana

CUBA

Gulf of Guacanayabo

CAYMAN IS. (U.K.)

TURKS & CAICOS IS. (U.K.)

Windward Passage

JAMAICA

Kingston

(U.S.)

HAITI

Port-au-Prince

DOMINICAN REPUBLIC

Santo Domingo

Mona Passage

PUERTO RICO (U.S.)

San Juan

(P.R.)

Caribbean Sea

NETHERLANDS ANTILLES (NETH.)

ARUBA (NETH.)

HONDURAS

NICARAGUA

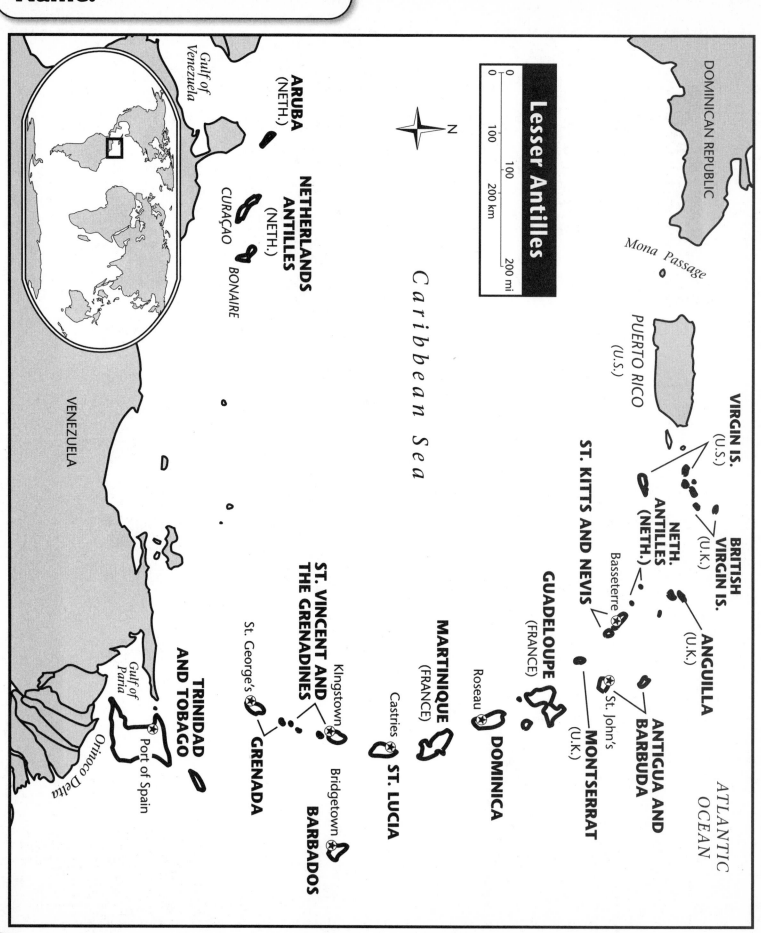

Lesser Antilles

0
0
100 100
100 200 km
200 mi

N

Gulf of Venezuela

ARUBA (NETH.)

CURAÇAO

NETHERLANDS ANTILLES (NETH.)

BONAIRE

VENEZUELA

Caribbean Sea

DOMINICAN REPUBLIC

Mona Passage

PUERTO RICO (U.S.)

VIRGIN IS. (U.S.)

BRITISH VIRGIN IS. (U.K.)

NETH. ANTILLES (NETH.)

ANGUILLA (U.K.)

ST. KITTS AND NEVIS

Basseterre

ST. JOHN'S

MONTSERRAT (U.K.)

ANTIGUA AND BARBUDA

GUADELOUPE (FRANCE)

Roseau

DOMINICA

MARTINIQUE (FRANCE)

Castries

ST. LUCIA

Bridgetown

BARBADOS

ST. VINCENT AND THE GRENADINES

Kingstown

St. George's

GRENADA

TRINIDAD AND TOBAGO

Port of Spain

Gulf of Paria

Orinoco Delta

ATLANTIC OCEAN

Caribbean Sea

ATLANTIC OCEAN

Lake Maracaibo
Orinoco
Magdalena
Meta
Caroní
Orinoco
Negro
Caquetá
Putumayo
Amazon
Tapajós
Xingu
Parnaíba
Purus
Madeira
Tocantins
Marañón
Guaporé
Araguaia
São Francisco
Ucayali
Lake Titicaca
Mamoré
Paraguay
Grande
Lake Poopó
Pilcomayo
Paraná
PACIFIC OCEAN
Salado
Uruguay
Desaguadero
Salado
Paraná
Río de la Plata
Colorado
ATLANTIC OCEAN
San Matías Gulf
Gulf of San Jorge
N
Bahía Grande
Strait of Magellan

South America

| 0 | 250 | 500 | 750 mi |
| 0 | 250 | 500 | 750 | 1000 km |

Caribbean Sea

Caracas

VENEZUELA

Bogotá

COLOMBIA

Georgetown
Paramaribo
GUYANA
Cayenne
SURINAME
FRENCH GUIANA
(Fr.)

ATLANTIC
OCEAN

Quito

ECUADOR

PERU

Lima

BRAZIL

Brasília

La Paz

BOLIVIA

Sucre

PACIFIC
OCEAN

PARAGUAY

Asunción

ARGENTINA

Santiago

URUGUAY

Buenos Aires

Montevideo

CHILE

ATLANTIC
OCEAN

San Matías Gulf

Gulf of San Jorge

N

Bahía
Grande

Strait of Magellan

South America

0	250	500	750 mi
0	250 500 750	1000 km	

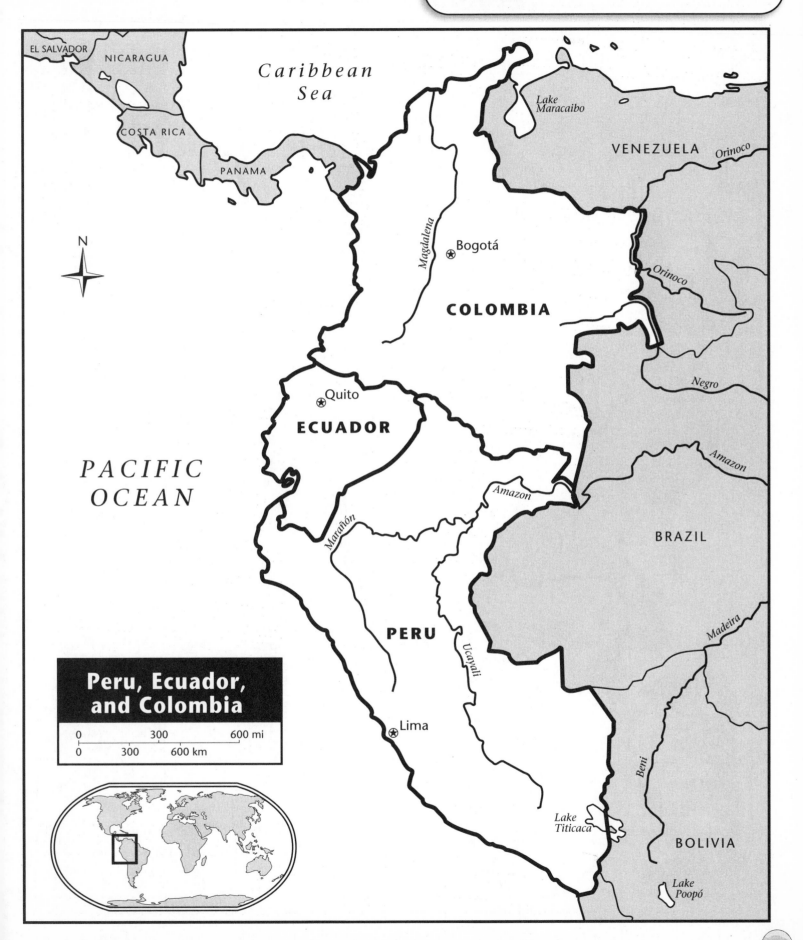

EL SALVADOR
NICARAGUA
Caribbean Sea
Lake Maracaibo
VENEZUELA
Orinoco
COSTA RICA
PANAMA
N
Magdalena
⊛ Bogotá
Orinoco
COLOMBIA
Negro
⊛ Quito
Amazon
ECUADOR
PACIFIC OCEAN
BRAZIL
Amazon
Marañón
Ucayali
PERU
Madeira

Peru, Ecuador, and Colombia

0	300	600 mi
0	300	600 km

⊛ Lima

Beni

Lake Titicaca

BOLIVIA

Lake Poopó

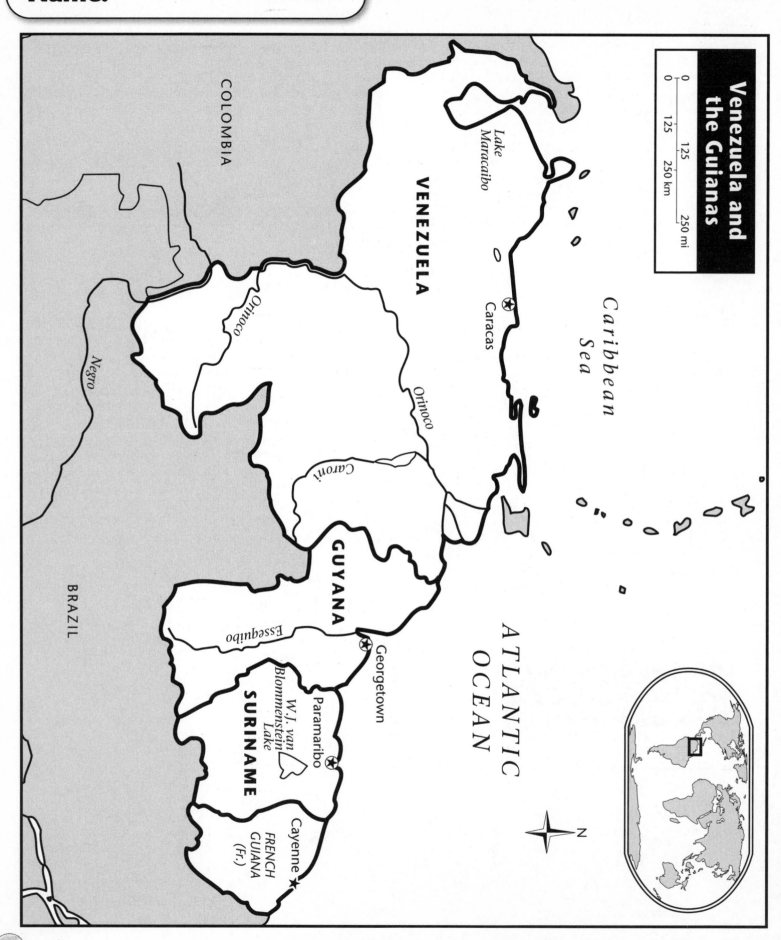

Venezuela and the Guianas

COLOMBIA

Lake Maracaibo

VENEZUELA

Orinoco

Caracas

Caribbean Sea

Orinoco

Caroní

Negro

BRAZIL

GUYANA

Essequibo

Georgetown

ATLANTIC OCEAN

W.J. van Blommenstein Lake

Paramaribo

SURINAME

Cayenne

FRENCH GUIANA (Fr.)

0   125   250 km
0   125   250 mi

N

Brazil and Bolivia

0   250   500 mi
0   250   500 km

Caribbean Sea

Lake Maracaibo

Orinoco

VENEZUELA

GUYANA

FRENCH GUIANA (FRANCE)

SURINAME

ATLANTIC OCEAN

N

COLOMBIA

Negro

Amazon

BRAZIL

Madeira

Tocantins

Ucayali

Beni

BOLIVIA

PERU

Lake Titicaca

⊛ La Paz

⊛ Brasília

Lake Poopó

Paraguay

PACIFIC OCEAN

PARAGUAY

CHILE

ARGENTINA

URUGUAY

Paraná

Río de la Plata

PERU

Lake Titicaca

Lake Poopó

BOLIVIA

Mamoré

Paraguay

BRAZIL

Grande

PARAGUAY

Pilcomayo

Paraná

Asunción

PACIFIC OCEAN

Desaguadero

Salado

Salado

Uruguay

Paraná

URUGUAY

Santiago

Buenos Aires

Montevideo

ARGENTINA

Río de la Plata

CHILE

Colorado

ATLANTIC OCEAN

Negro

San Matías Gulf

Chubut

Chico

Gulf of San Jorge

Bahía Grande

FALKLAND ISLANDS (UK)

Strait of Magellan

N

Argentina, Chile, Paraguay, and Uruguay

0		250		500 mi
0	250		500 km	

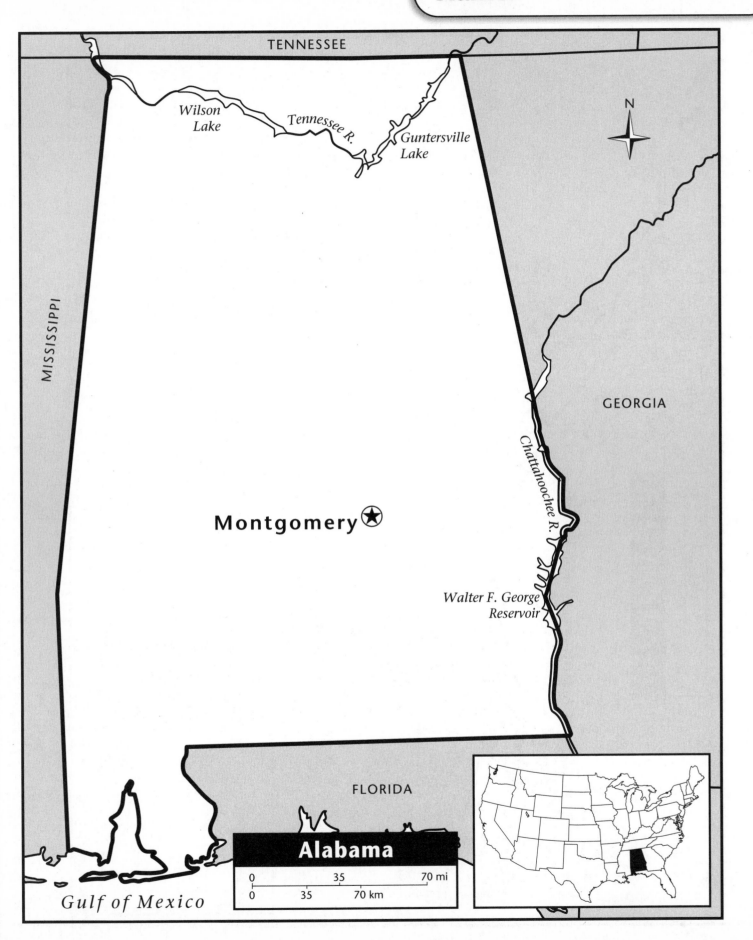

TENNESSEE

Wilson Lake

Tennessee R.

Guntersville Lake

N

MISSISSIPPI

GEORGIA

Chattahoochee R.

Montgomery ★

Walter F. George Reservoir

FLORIDA

Alabama

0   35   70 mi

0   35   70 km

Gulf of Mexico

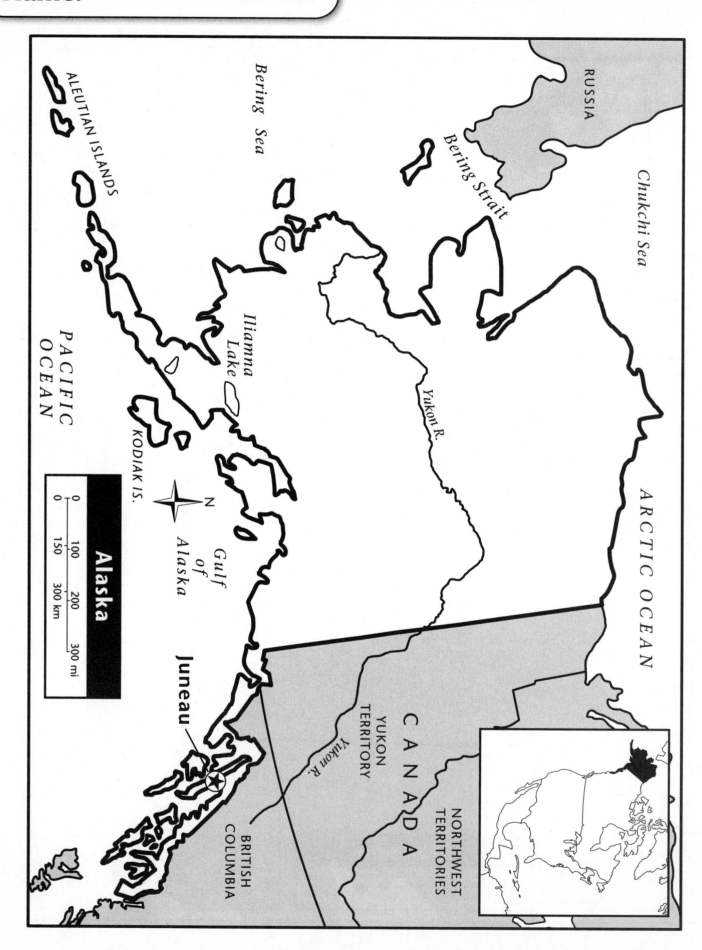

Alaska

ALEUTIAN ISLANDS

Bering Sea

Bering Strait

RUSSIA

Chukchi Sea

Iliamna Lake

PACIFIC OCEAN

Yukon R.

ARCTIC OCEAN

KODIAK IS.

N

Gulf of Alaska

0 0
0 150 300 km
0 100 200 300 mi

Juneau

BRITISH COLUMBIA

Yukon R.

YUKON TERRITORY

CANADA

NORTHWEST TERRITORIES

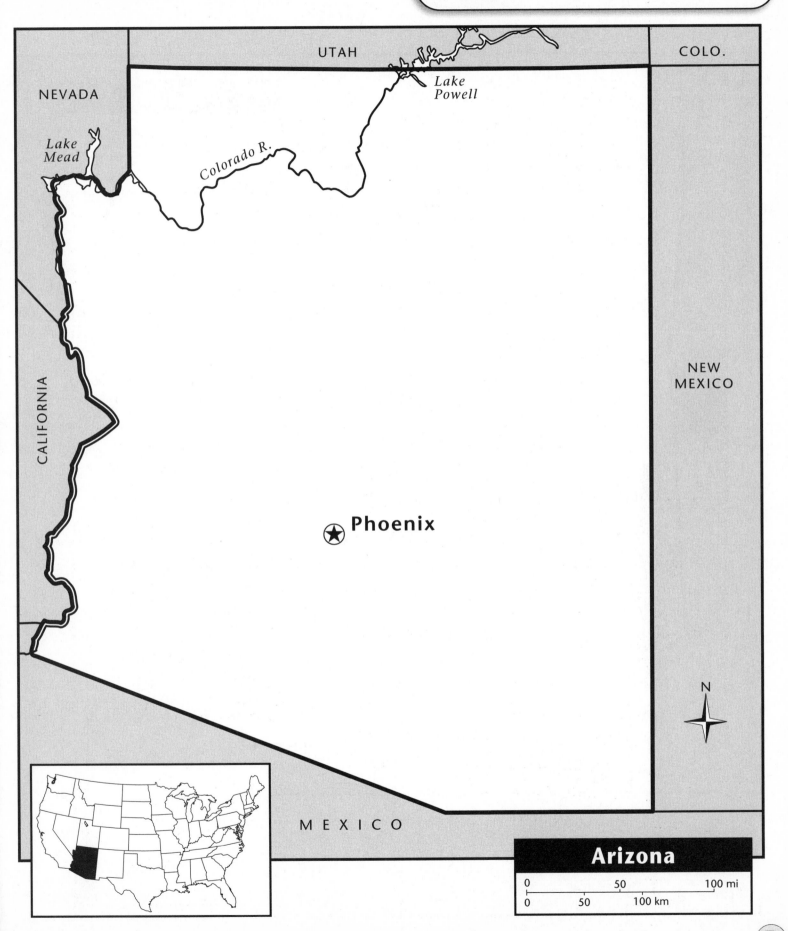

Name:

COLO.

UTAH

NEVADA

Lake Powell

Lake Mead

Colorado R.

CALIFORNIA

NEW MEXICO

★ **Phoenix**

N

MEXICO

Arizona

| 0 | | 50 | | 100 mi |
| 0 | 50 | | 100 km | |

KANSAS

MISSOURI

Arkansas

| 0 | 35 | 70 mi |
| 0 | 35 | 70 km |

Beaver
Lake

Bull Shoals
Lake

White R.

Lake
Dardanelle

Arkansas R.

Mississippi R.

TENN.

OKLA.

★ **Little Rock**

N

TEXAS

MISSISSIPPI

LOUISIANA

N

OREGON

Klamath R.   Goose L.

UTAH

Sacramento R.

Pyramid L.

NEVADA

L. Tahoe

⭐ **Sacramento**

San Joaquin R.

PACIFIC
OCEAN

L. Mead

ARIZ.

California

| 0 | 75 | 150 mi |
| 0 | 75 | 150 km |

Colorado R.

CHANNEL ISLANDS

Salton
Sea

MEXICO

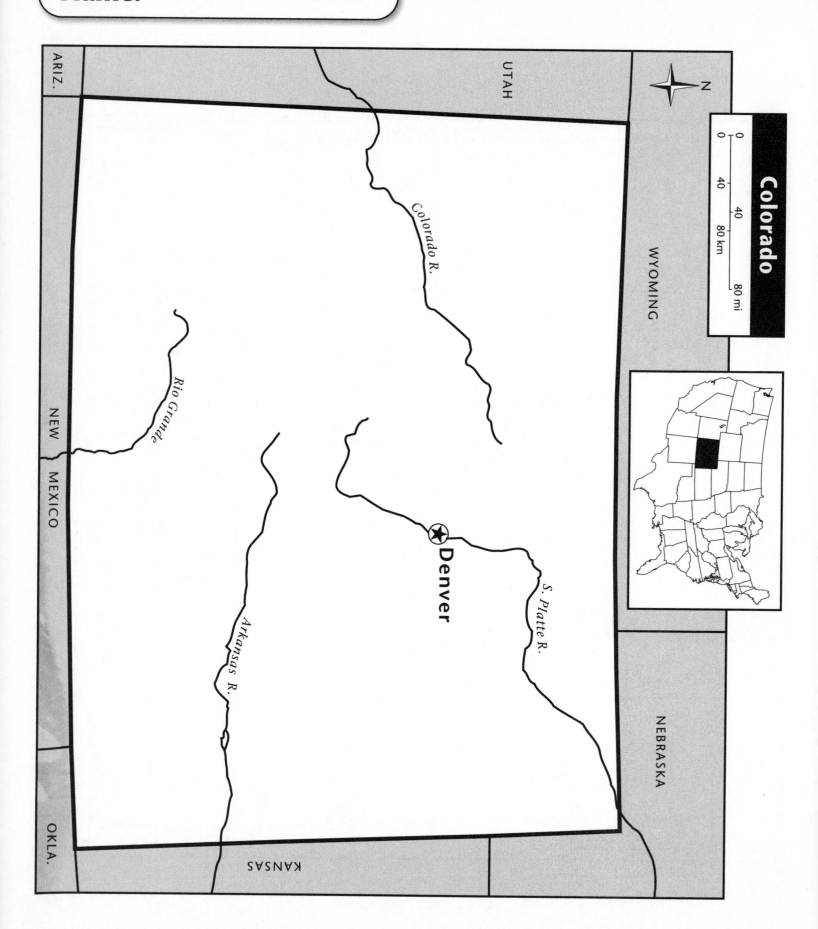

Name:

Colorado

ARIZ.

UTAH

N

Colorado R.

WYOMING

0
0
40
40
80 km
80 mi

NEW
MEXICO

Rio Grande

Denver

S. Platte R.

Arkansas R.

NEBRASKA

OKLA.

KANSAS

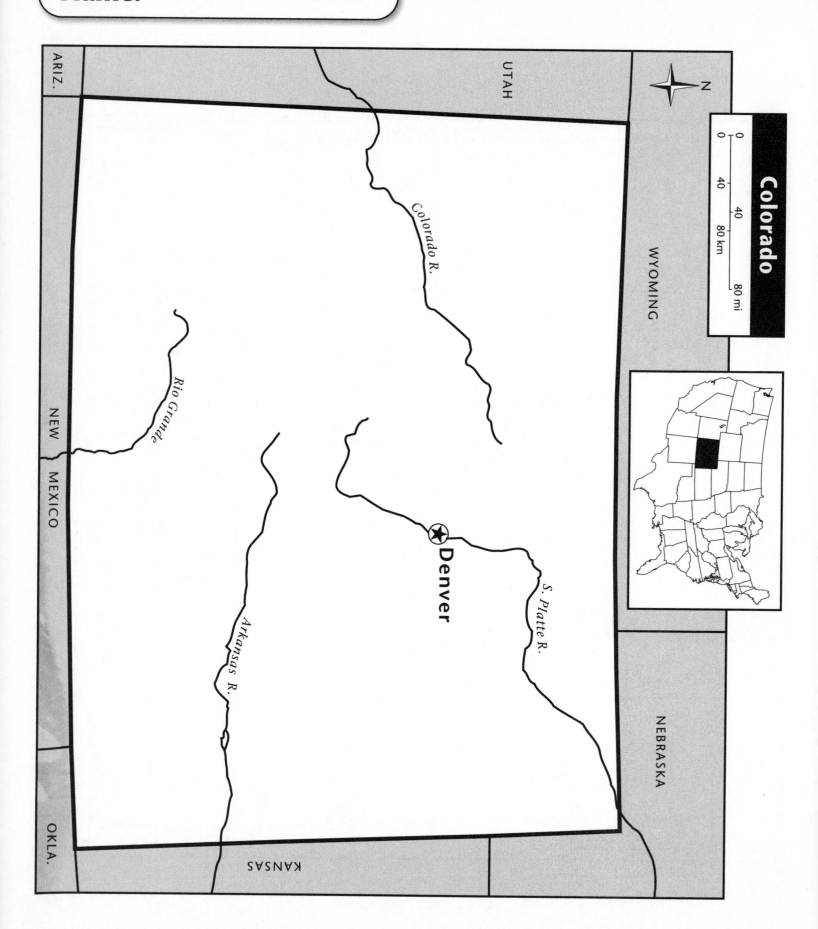

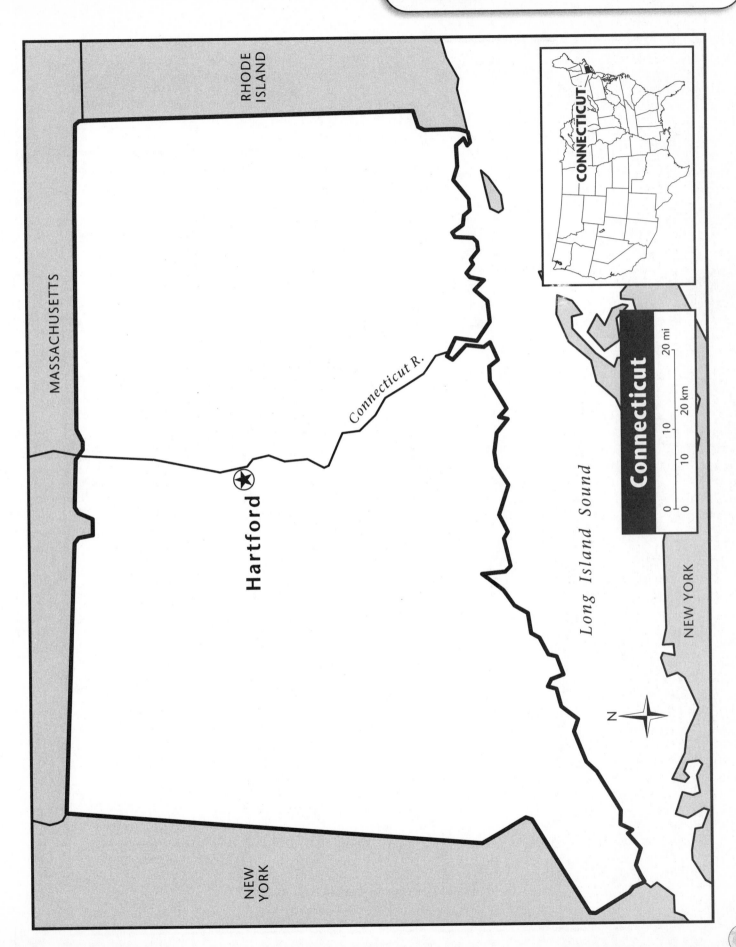

RHODE ISLAND

MASSACHUSETTS

NEW YORK

NEW YORK

Connecticut R.

Hartford

Long Island Sound

CONNECTICUT

Connecticut

20 mi

10

20 km

10

0

0

N

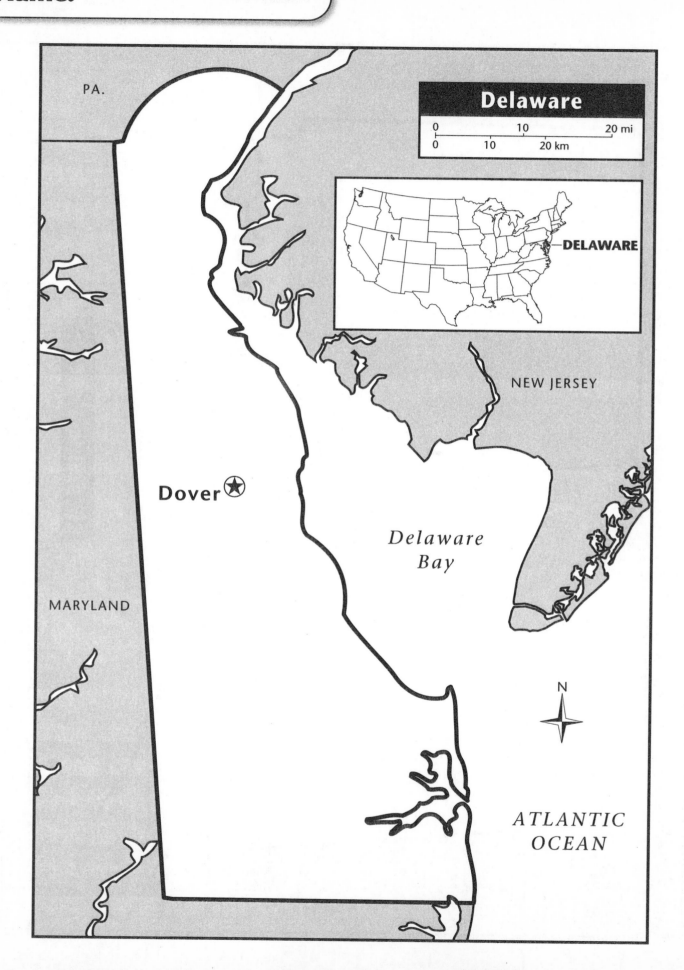

Delaware

0   10   20 mi
0   10   20 km

DELAWARE

PA.

NEW JERSEY

Dover ★

MARYLAND

Delaware
Bay

N

ATLANTIC
OCEAN

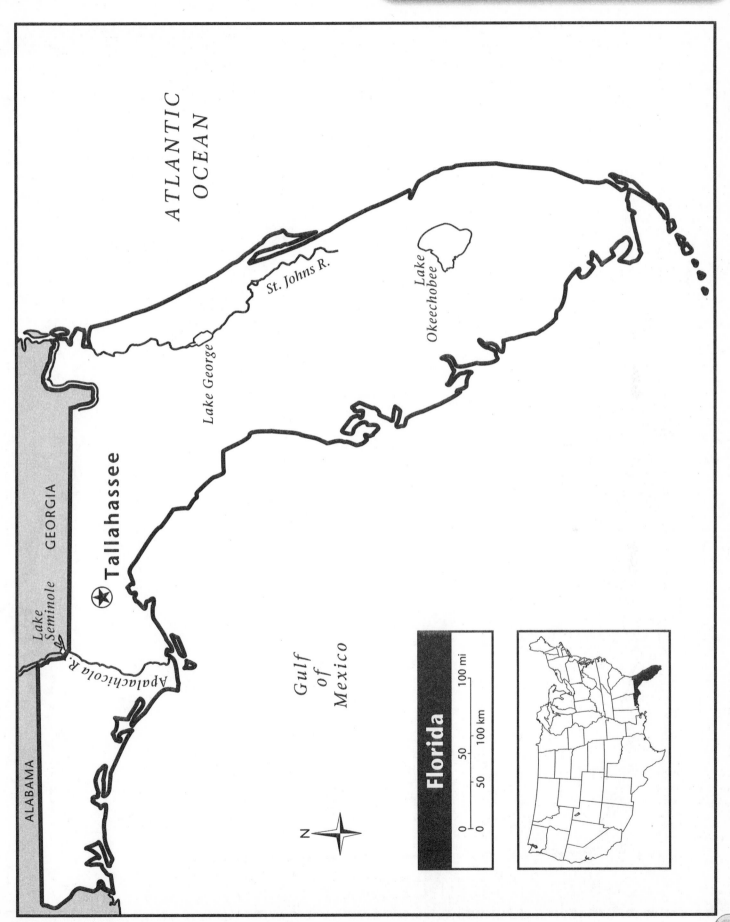

ATLANTIC OCEAN

St. Johns R.

Lake George

Lake Okeechobee

Tallahassee

GEORGIA

ALABAMA

Lake Seminole

Apalachicola R.

Gulf of Mexico

Florida

100 mi

50   100 km

0   50

0

N

TENNESSEE

N.C.

Georgia

0   35   70 mi
0   35   70 km

Hartwell
Lake

Lake Sidney
Lanier

★ **Atlanta**

Strom Thurmond
Reservoir

SOUTH
CAROLINA

Savannah R.

West Point
Lake

Chattahoochee R.

ALABAMA

Walter F. George
Reservoir

ATLANTIC OCEAN

N

Lake
Seminole

FLORIDA

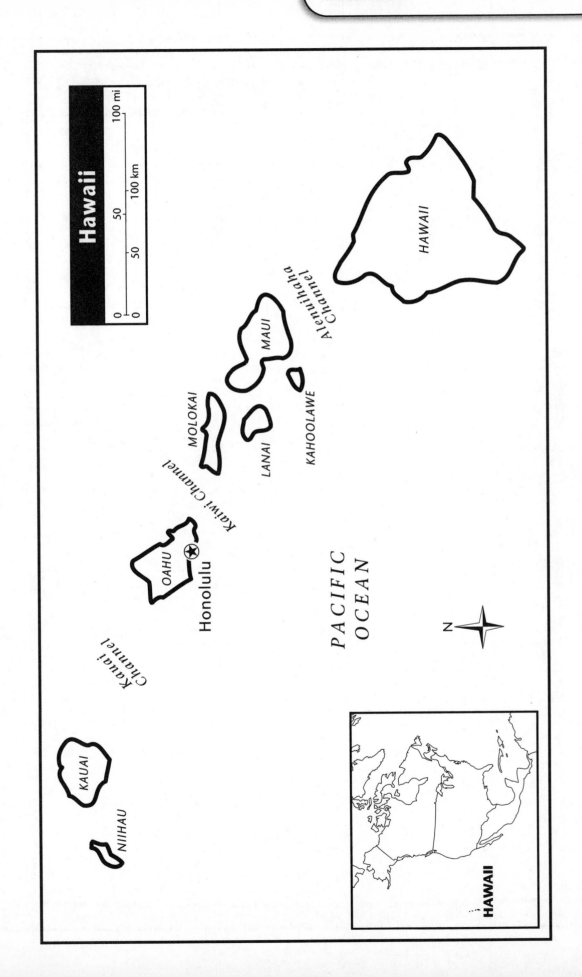

Hawaii

100 mi

100 km

50

50

50

0

0

HAWAII

MAUI

Alenuihaha Channel

MOLOKAI

LANAI

KAHOOLAWE

Kaiwi Channel

OAHU

Honolulu

Kauai Channel

KAUAI

NIIHAU

PACIFIC OCEAN

N

HAWAII

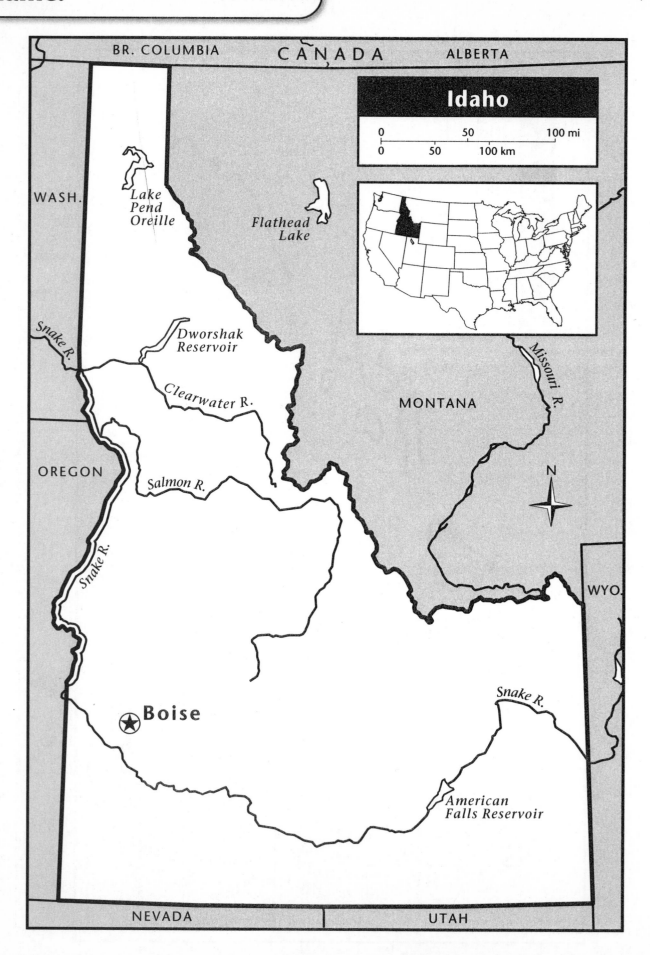

CANADA

BR. COLUMBIA

ALBERTA

Idaho

0   50   100 mi
0   50   100 km

WASH.

Lake Pend Oreille

Flathead Lake

Snake R.

Dworshak Reservoir

Clearwater R.

MONTANA

Missouri R.

OREGON

Salmon R.

N

Snake R.

WYO.

Snake R.

★ Boise

American Falls Reservoir

NEVADA

UTAH

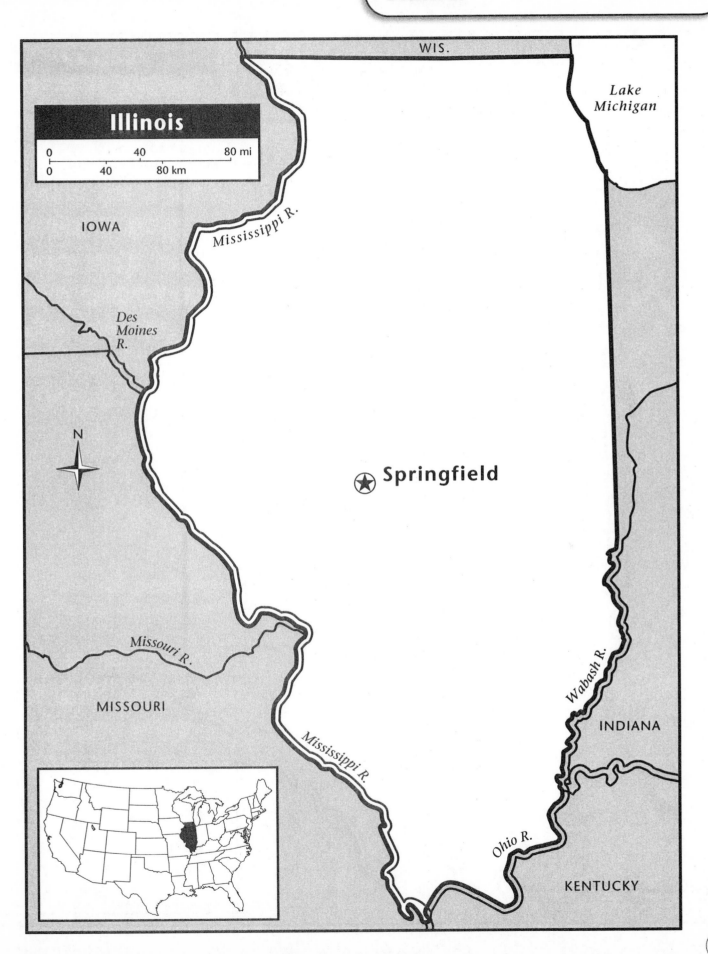

Illinois

0 — 40 — 80 mi
0 — 40 — 80 km

WIS.

Lake Michigan

IOWA

Mississippi R.

Des Moines R.

N

★ **Springfield**

Missouri R.

MISSOURI

Mississippi R.

Wabash R.

INDIANA

Ohio R.

KENTUCKY

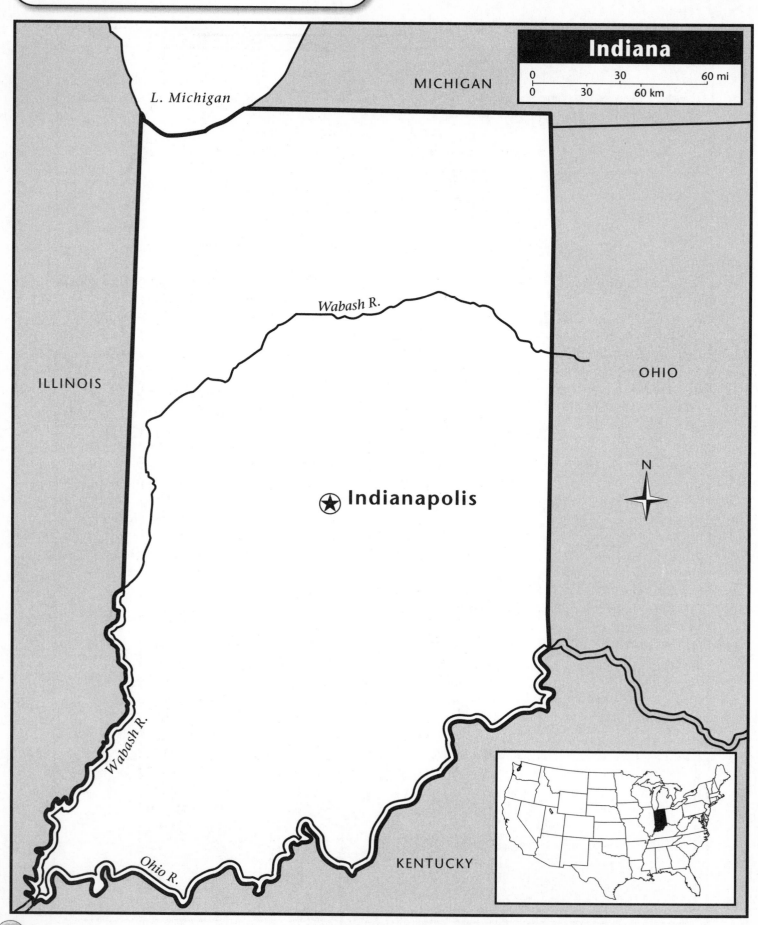

Indiana

0   30   60 mi
0   30   60 km

MICHIGAN

L. Michigan

ILLINOIS

Wabash R.

OHIO

N

⊛ **Indianapolis**

Wabash R.

Ohio R.

KENTUCKY

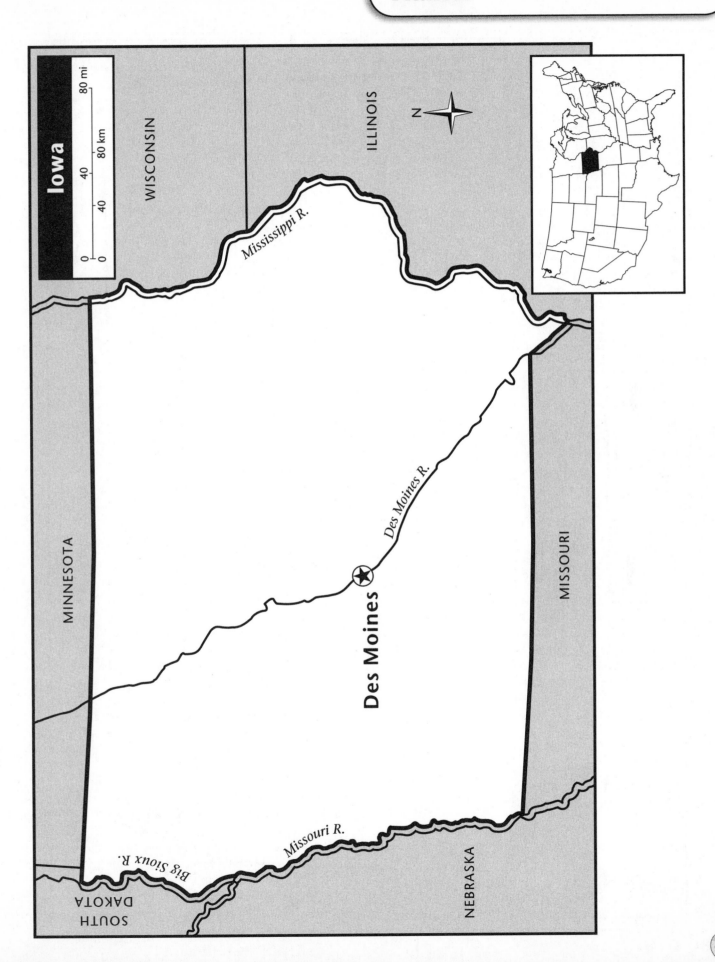

Iowa

80 mi
40   80 km
0   40
0   80

WISCONSIN

ILLINOIS

N

Mississippi R.

MINNESOTA

Des Moines R.

★ Des Moines

MISSOURI

Missouri R.

Big Sioux R.

SOUTH DAKOTA

NEBRASKA

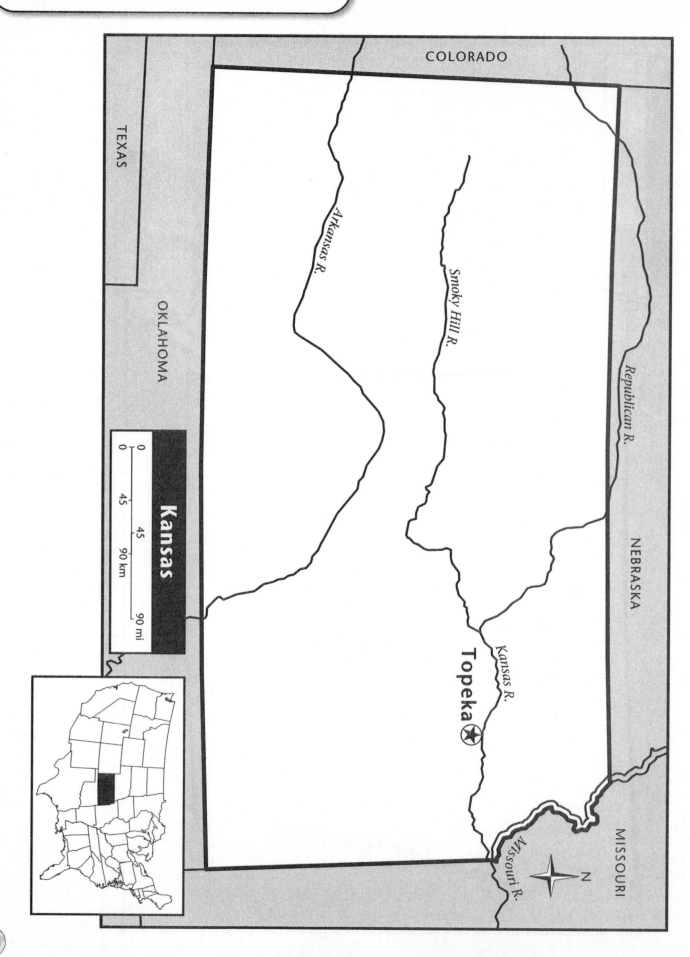

COLORADO

TEXAS

OKLAHOMA

Arkansas R.

Smoky Hill R.

Republican R.

NEBRASKA

Kansas R.

Topeka

0
0
45
45
45
90 km
90 mi

Kansas

Missouri R.

MISSOURI

N

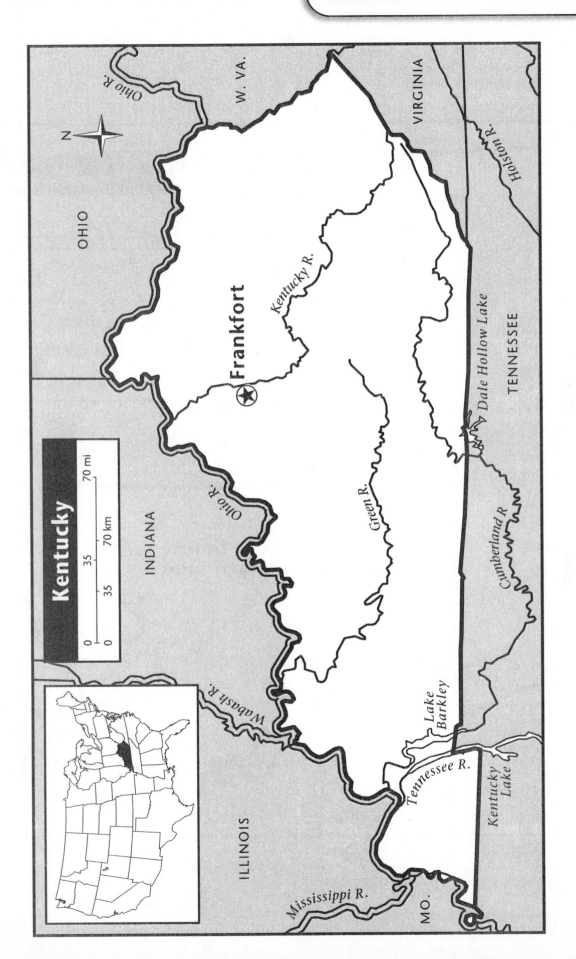

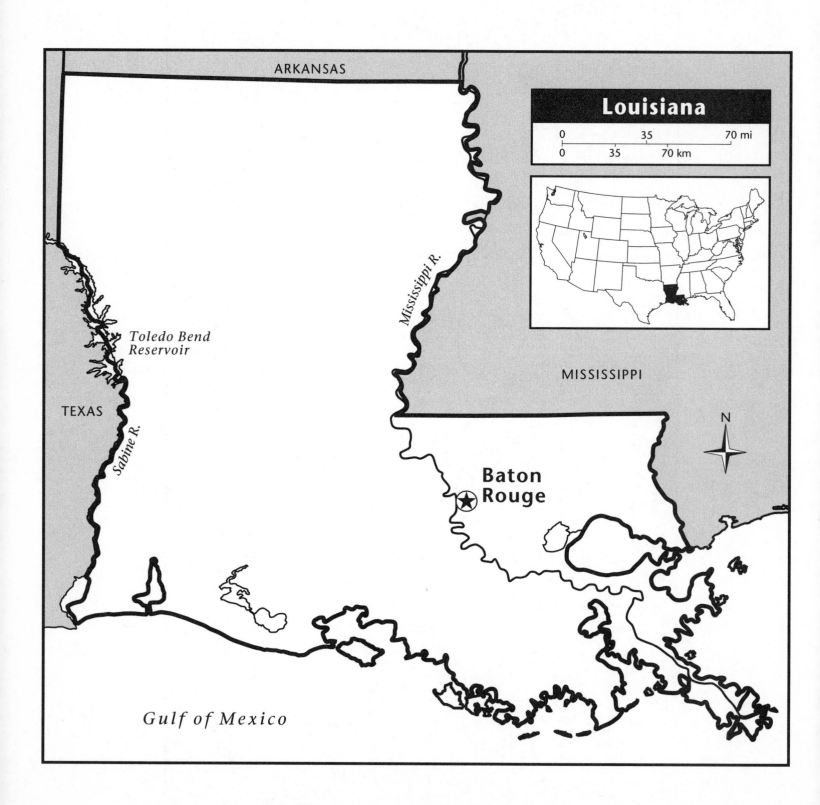

ARKANSAS

Louisiana

| 0 | | 35 | | 70 mi |
| 0 | | 35 | 70 km | |

Toledo Bend
Reservoir

Mississippi R.

MISSISSIPPI

TEXAS

Sabine R.

N

**Baton
Rouge**

Gulf of Mexico

Maine

0 30 60 mi
0 30 60 km

St. Lawrence R.

C A N A D A

QUEBEC

NEW BRUNSWICK

Saint John R.

Penobscot R.

Grand Lake

Augusta ★

N.H.

N

ATLANTIC OCEAN

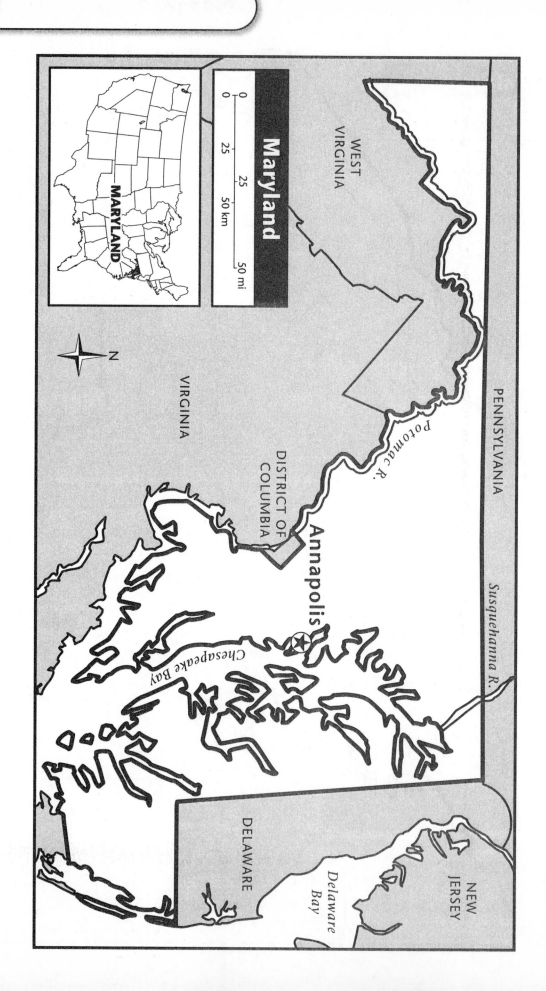

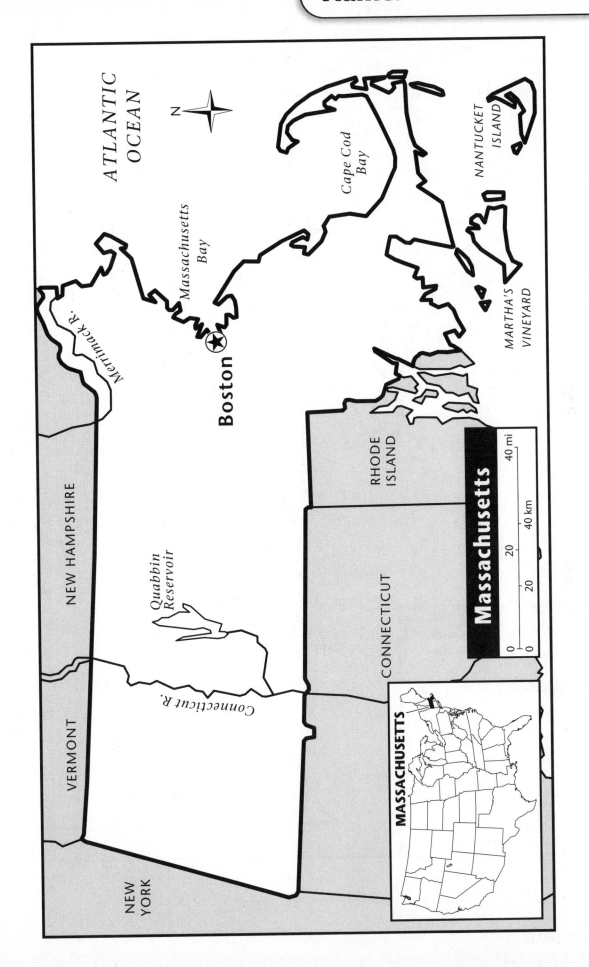

ATLANTIC OCEAN

N

Cape Cod Bay

NANTUCKET ISLAND

Massachusetts Bay

Merrimack R.

MARTHA'S VINEYARD

Boston

NEW HAMPSHIRE

RHODE ISLAND

Quabbin Reservoir

CONNECTICUT

Massachusetts

0	20	40 mi
0	20	40 km

Connecticut R.

VERMONT

NEW YORK

MASSACHUSETTS

N

KEWEENAW
PENINSULA

Lake Superior

CANADA

ONTARIO

Menominee R.

Wisconsin R.

Green Bay

WISCONSIN

*L.
Winnebago*

*Lake
Michigan*

*Lake
Huron*

Saginaw Bay

Muskegon R.

Grand R.

⭐ **Lansing**

Michigan

0	50	100 mi
0	50	100 km

INDIANA

OHIO

*Lake
Erie*

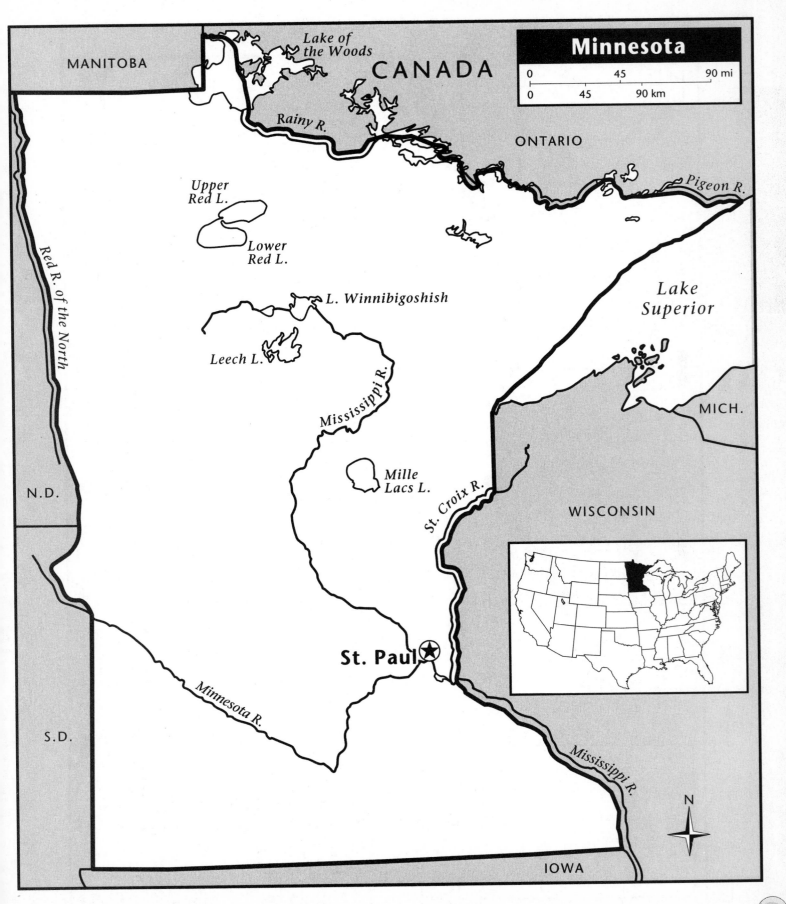

MANITOBA

CANADA

Lake of the Woods

ONTARIO

Minnesota

0   45   90 mi

0   45   90 km

Rainy R.

Pigeon R.

Upper Red L.

Lower Red L.

L. Winnibigoshish

Red R. of the North

Leech L.

Mississippi R.

Lake Superior

MICH.

N.D.

Mille Lacs L.

St. Croix R.

WISCONSIN

St. Paul ★

S.D.

Minnesota R.

Mississippi R.

N

IOWA

Name:

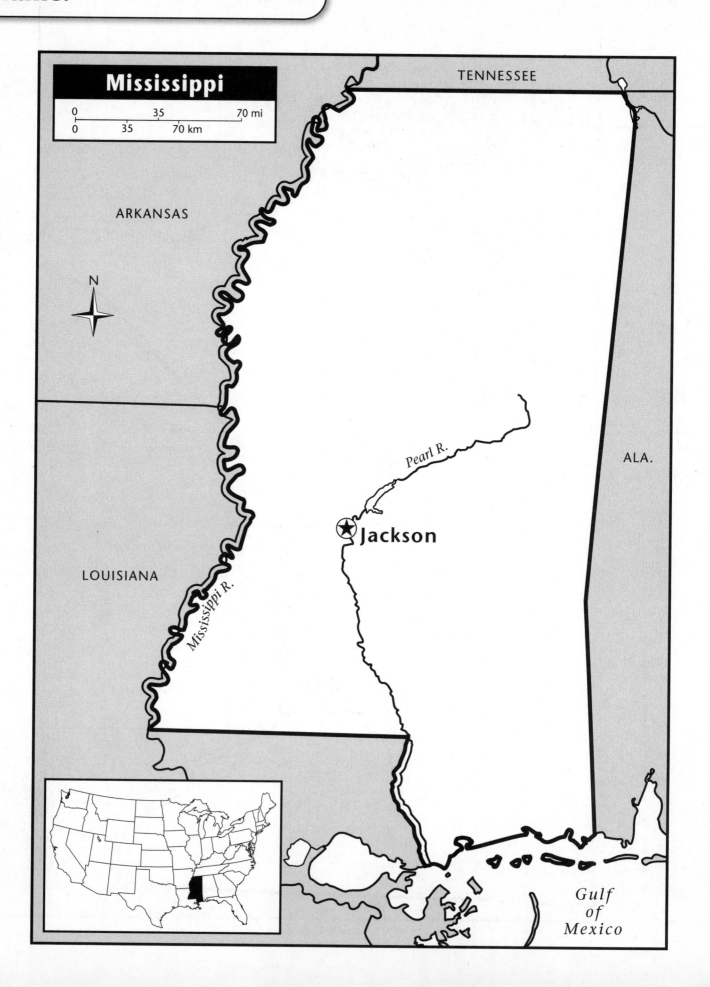

Mississippi

0   35   70 mi
0   35   70 km

TENNESSEE

ARKANSAS

N

LOUISIANA

Mississippi R.

Pearl R.

★ Jackson

ALA.

Gulf
of
Mexico

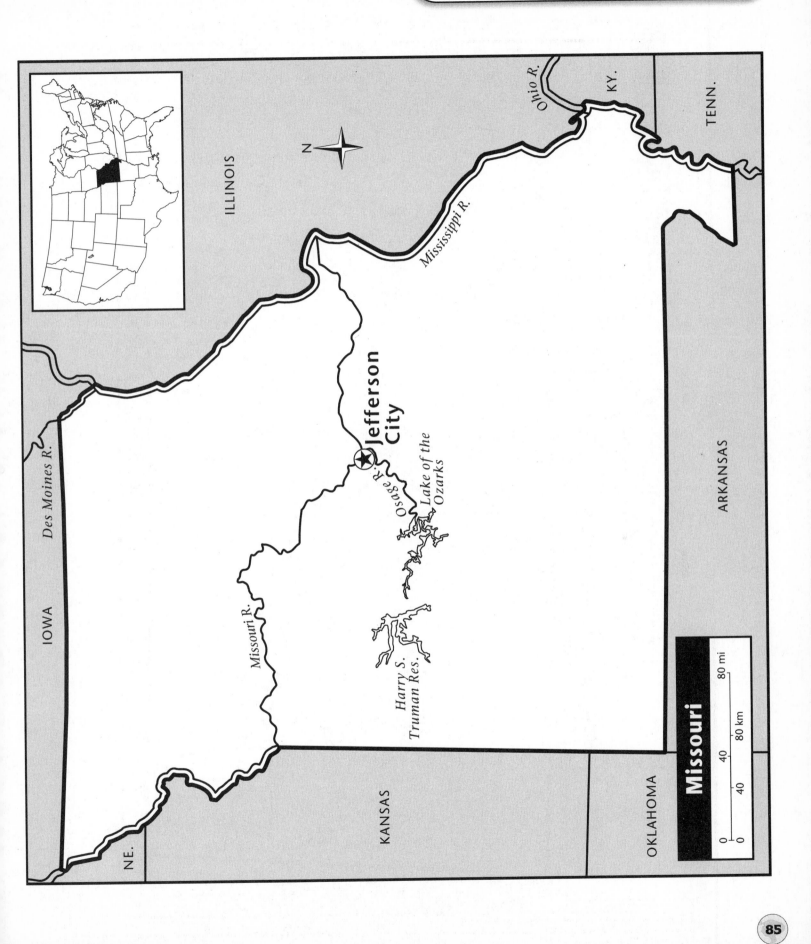

ILLINOIS

N

Ohio R.

KY.

TENN.

Mississippi R.

Des Moines R.

ARKANSAS

Jefferson
City

Osage R.

Lake of the
Ozarks

IOWA

Missouri R.

Harry S.
Truman Res.

NE.

KANSAS

OKLAHOMA

Missouri

0	40	80 mi
0	40	80 km

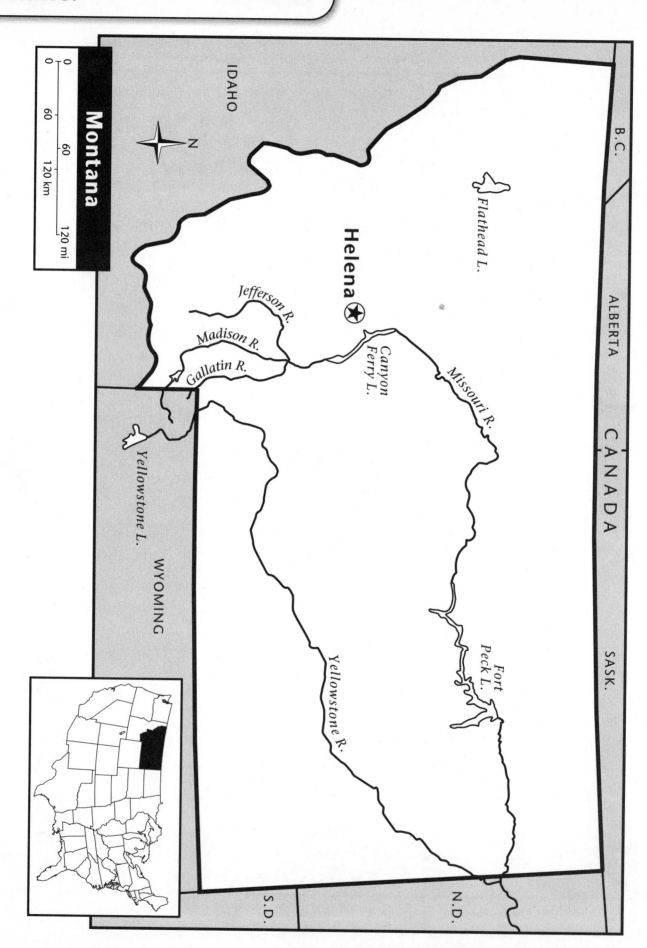

Montana

0
0
60
60
60
120 km
120 mi

N

IDAHO

B.C.

ALBERTA

CANADA

SASK.

Flathead L.

Helena ★

Jefferson R.

Madison R.

Gallatin R.

Canyon Ferry L.

Missouri R.

Yellowstone L.

Fort Peck L.

WYOMING

Yellowstone R.

S.D.

N.D.

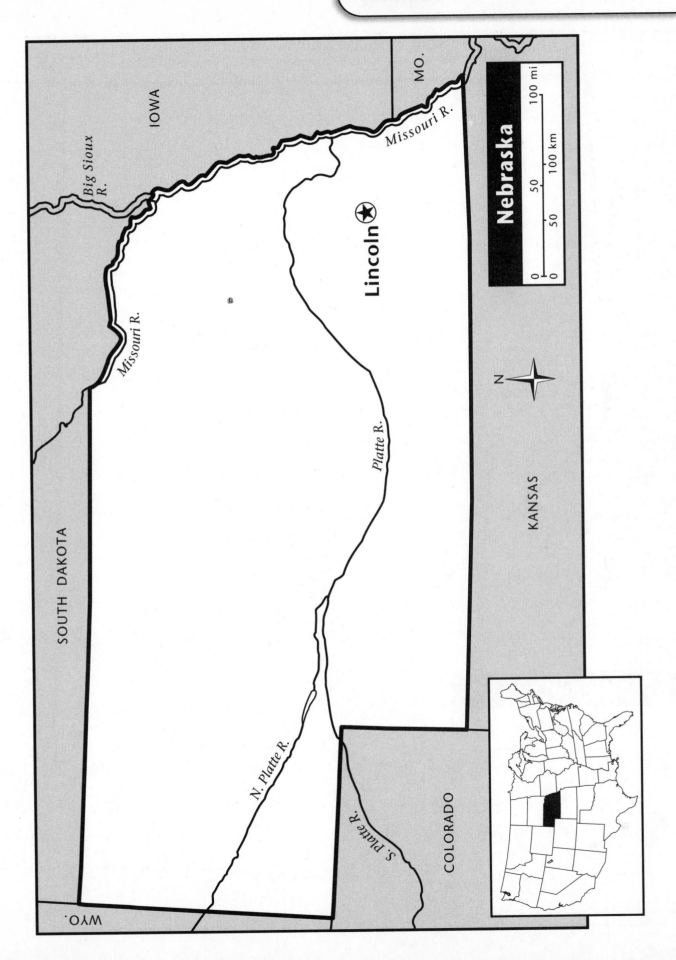

Nebraska

100 mi
50
0
100 km
50
0

MO.

IOWA

Missouri R.

Big Sioux R.

Missouri R.

Lincoln ✪

N

SOUTH DAKOTA

Platte R.

KANSAS

N. Platte R.

S. Platte R.

COLORADO

WYO.

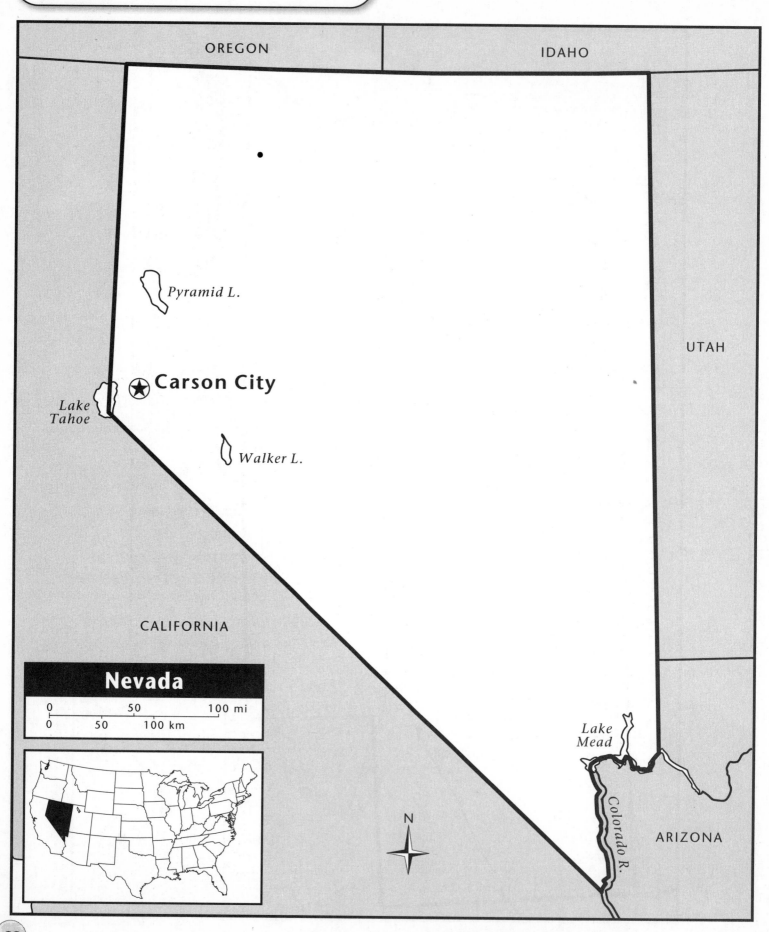

Name:

OREGON

IDAHO

UTAH

Pyramid L.

⭐ **Carson City**

Lake Tahoe

Walker L.

CALIFORNIA

Nevada

0   50   100 mi
0   50   100 km

Lake Mead

N

Colorado R.

ARIZONA

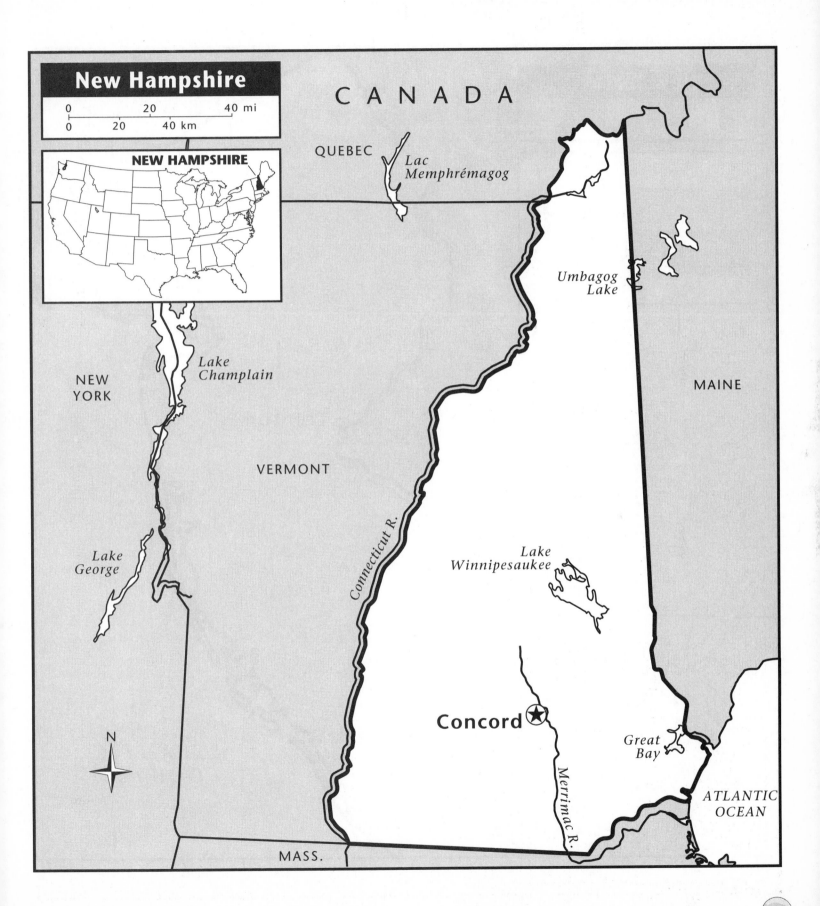

New Hampshire

0   20   40 mi
0   20   40 km

NEW HAMPSHIRE

CANADA

QUEBEC

Lac Memphrémagog

Umbagog Lake

MAINE

NEW YORK

Lake Champlain

VERMONT

Lake George

Connecticut R.

Lake Winnipesaukee

N

Concord ★

Great Bay

Merrimac R.

ATLANTIC OCEAN

MASS.

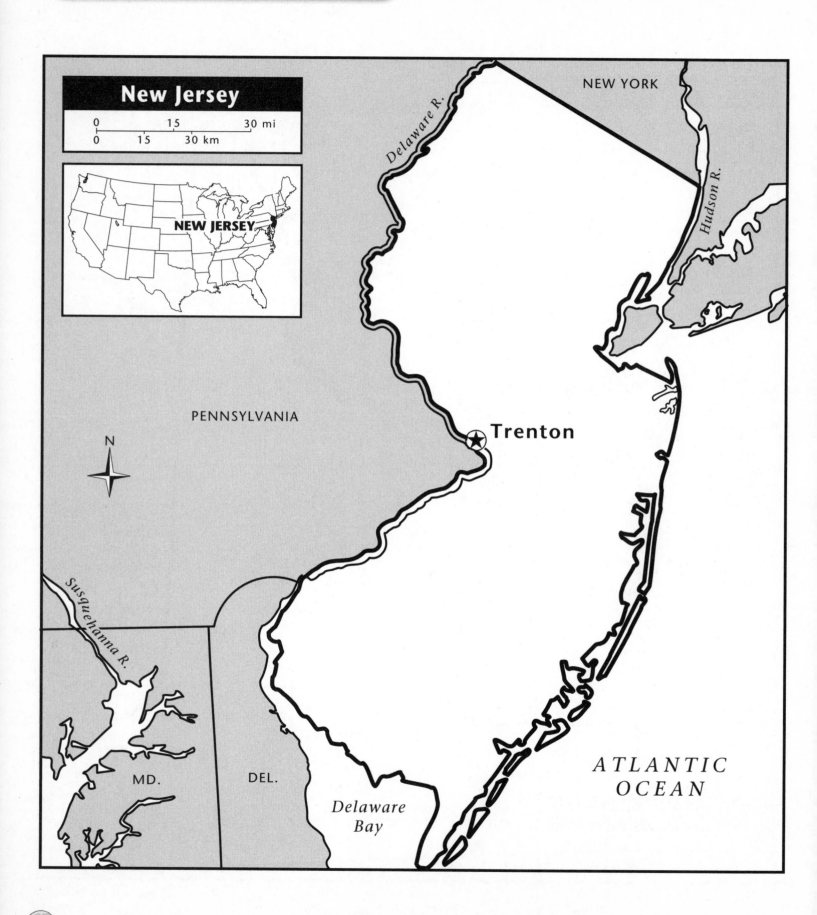

New Jersey

0   15   30 mi
0   15   30 km

NEW JERSEY

NEW YORK

Delaware R.

Hudson R.

N

PENNSYLVANIA

★ Trenton

Susquehanna R.

MD.

DEL.

Delaware
Bay

ATLANTIC
OCEAN

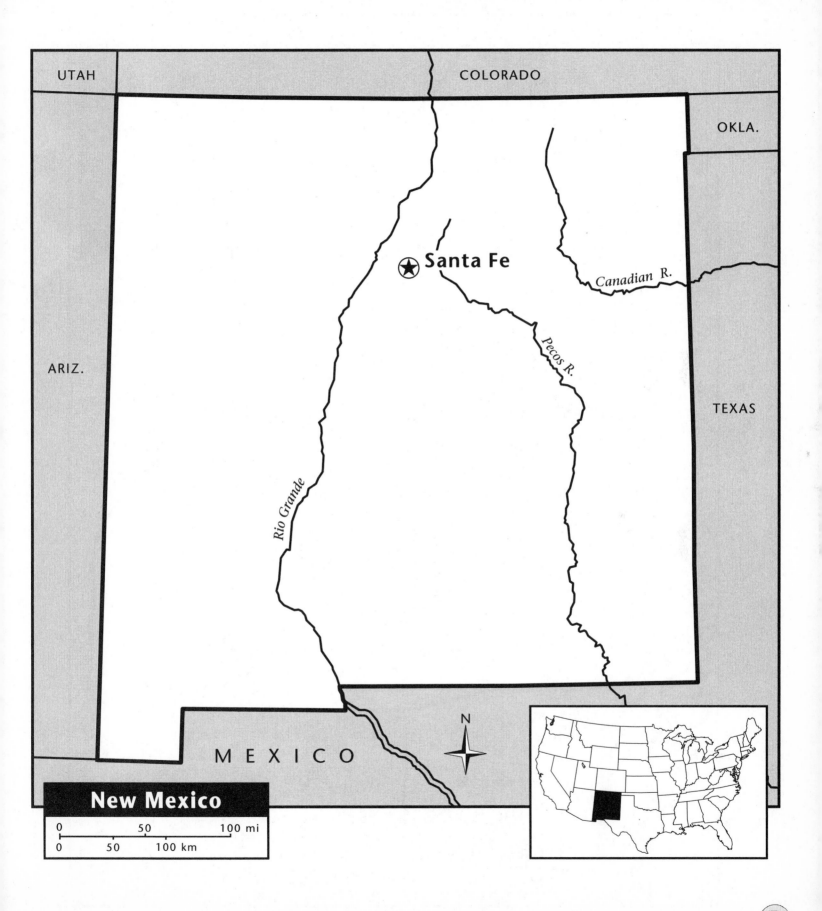

UTAH

COLORADO

OKLA.

ARIZ.

★ Santa Fe

Canadian R.

Pecos R.

TEXAS

Rio Grande

N

M E X I C O

New Mexico

| 0 | 50 | 100 mi |
| 0 | 50 | 100 km |

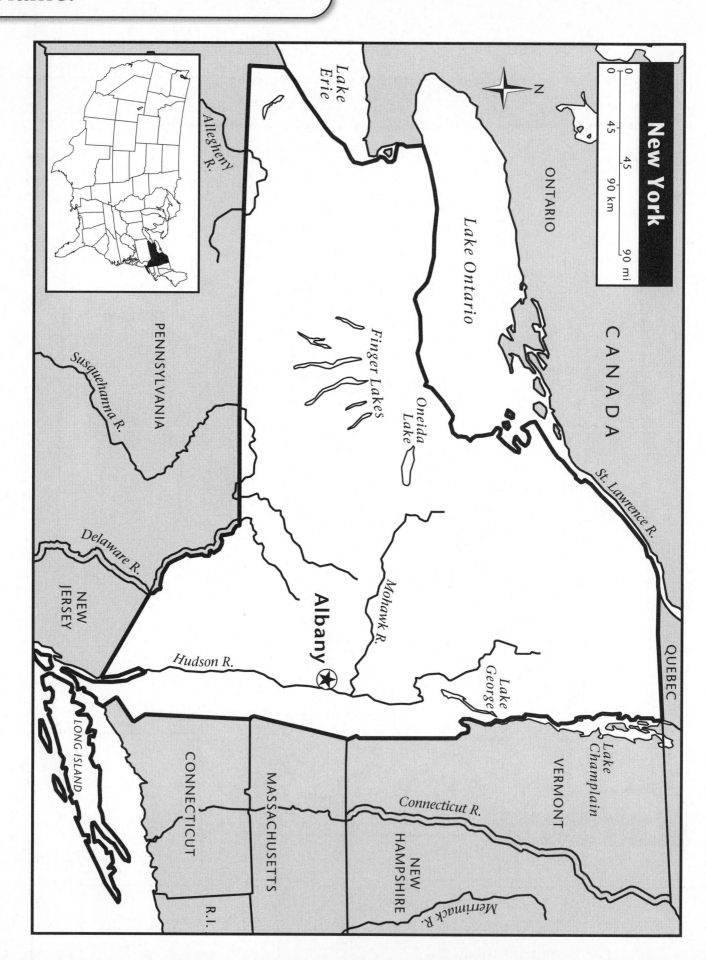

New York

ONTARIO

CANADA

Lake
Erie

Lake Ontario

PENNSYLVANIA

Allegheny
R.

Susquehanna R.

Finger Lakes

Oneida
Lake

St. Lawrence R.

Delaware R.

NEW
JERSEY

Hudson R.

Albany

Mohawk R.

QUEBEC

Lake
George

Lake
Champlain

VERMONT

LONG ISLAND

CONNECTICUT

MASSACHUSETTS

Connecticut R.

NEW
HAMPSHIRE

R.I.

Merrimack R.

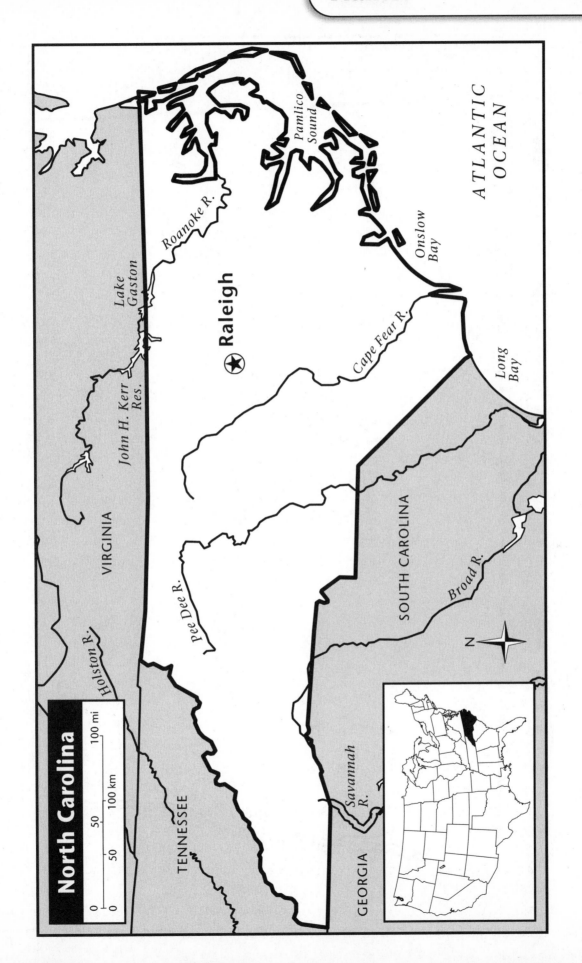

North Carolina

100 mi
50
0

100 km
50
0

ATLANTIC OCEAN

Pamlico Sound

Onslow Bay

Roanoke R.

Lake Gaston

Raleigh

Cape Fear R.

Long Bay

John H. Kerr Res.

VIRGINIA

SOUTH CAROLINA

Broad R.

Holston R.

Pee Dee R.

TENNESSEE

Savannah R.

GEORGIA

N

93

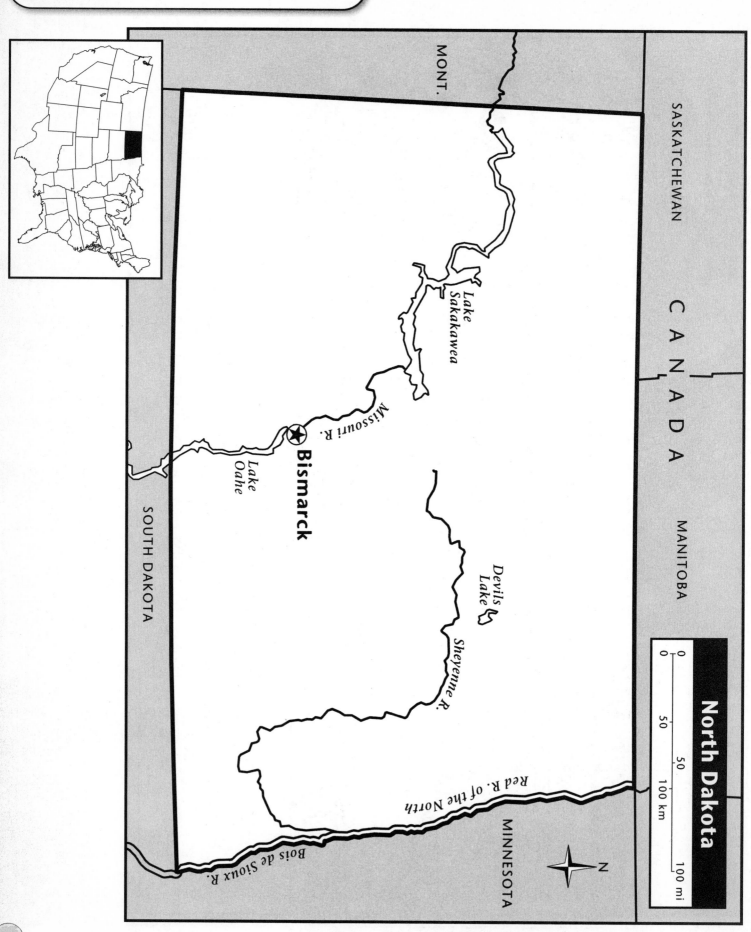

MONT.

SASKATCHEWAN

C A N A D A

MANITOBA

Lake
Sakakawea

Missouri R.

Bismarck

Lake
Oahe

SOUTH DAKOTA

Devils
Lake

Sheyenne R.

Red R. of the North

Bois de Sioux R.

MINNESOTA

North Dakota

0
0
50
50
100 km
100 mi

N

Name:

CANADA

MICHIGAN

IND.

PA.

Sandusky R.

⭐ **Columbus**

Ohio R.

N

WEST VIRGINIA

Ohio R.

KENTUCKY

Ohio

0   30   60 mi
0   30   60 km

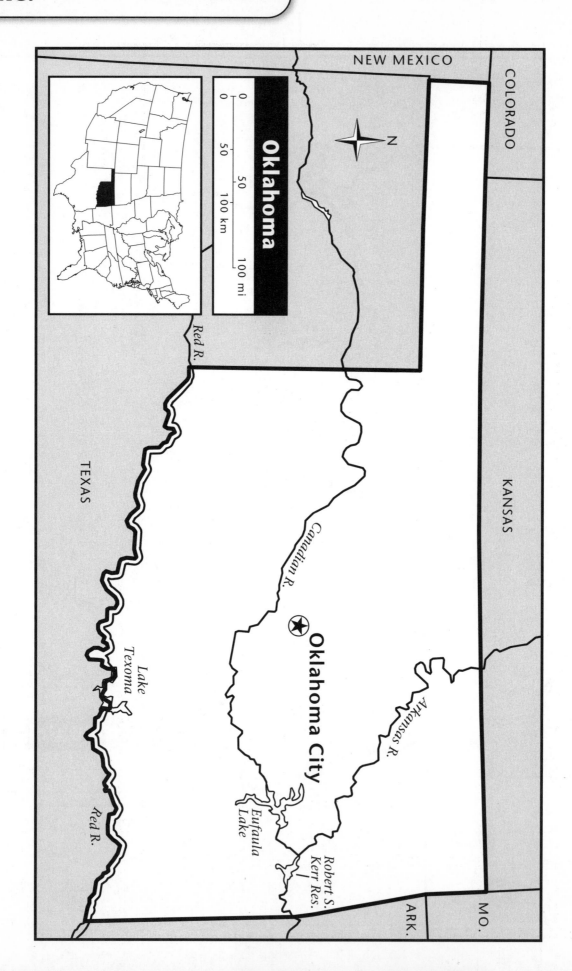

Oklahoma

NEW MEXICO

COLORADO

KANSAS

TEXAS

Red R.

Canadian R.

★ Oklahoma City

Lake Texoma

Arkansas R.

Red R.

Eufaula Lake

Robert S. Kerr Res.

ARK.

MO.

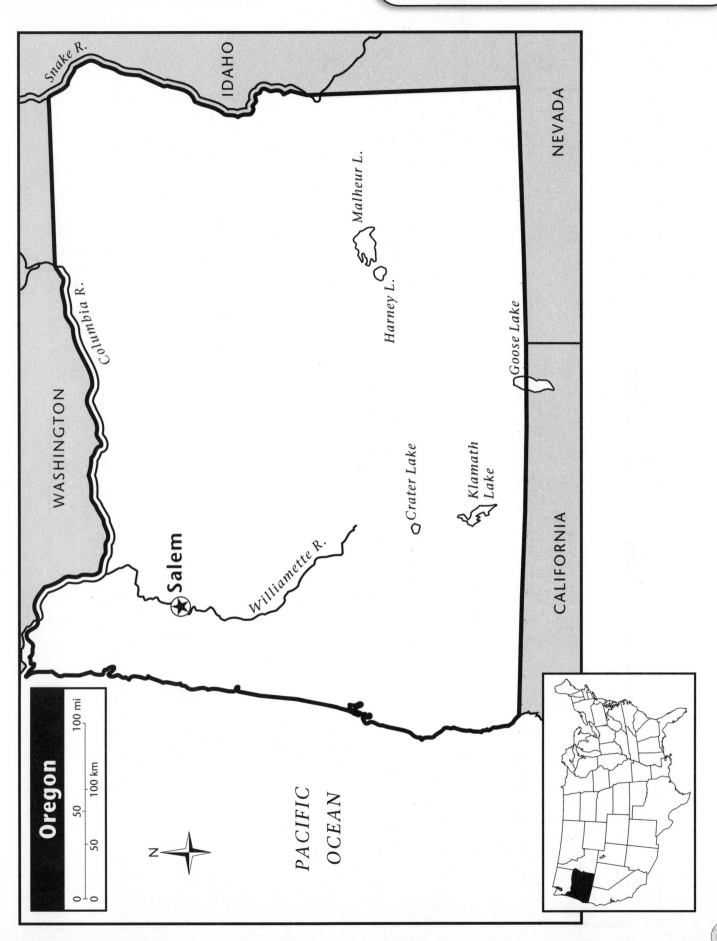

IDAHO

Snake R.

NEVADA

Malheur L.

Harney L.

Goose Lake

Columbia R.

WASHINGTON

Crater Lake

Klamath Lake

CALIFORNIA

Salem

Williamette R.

Oregon

100 mi

100 km

50

50

N

PACIFIC OCEAN

0

0

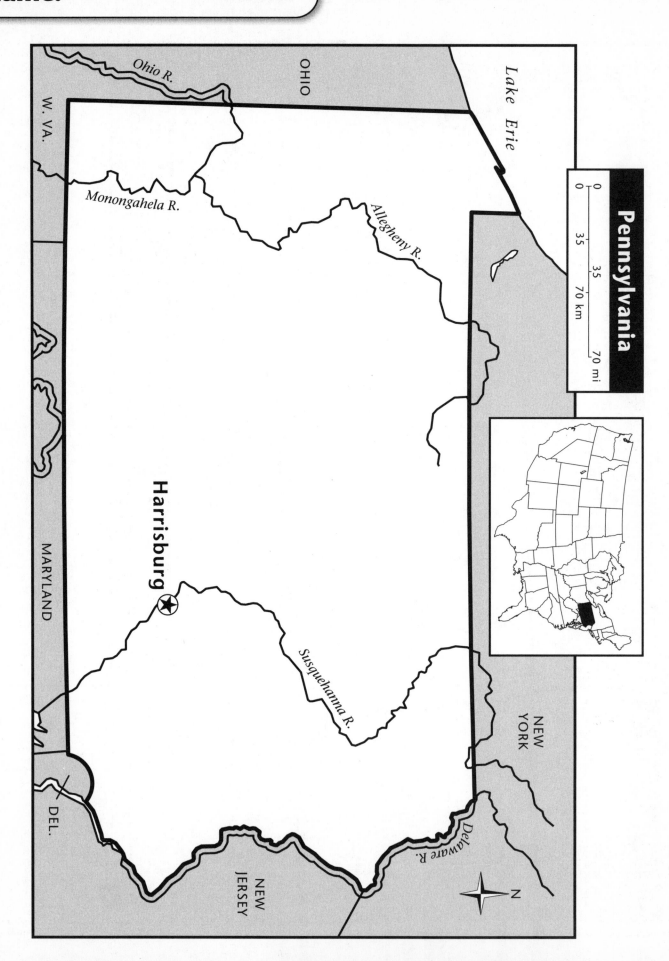

Pennsylvania

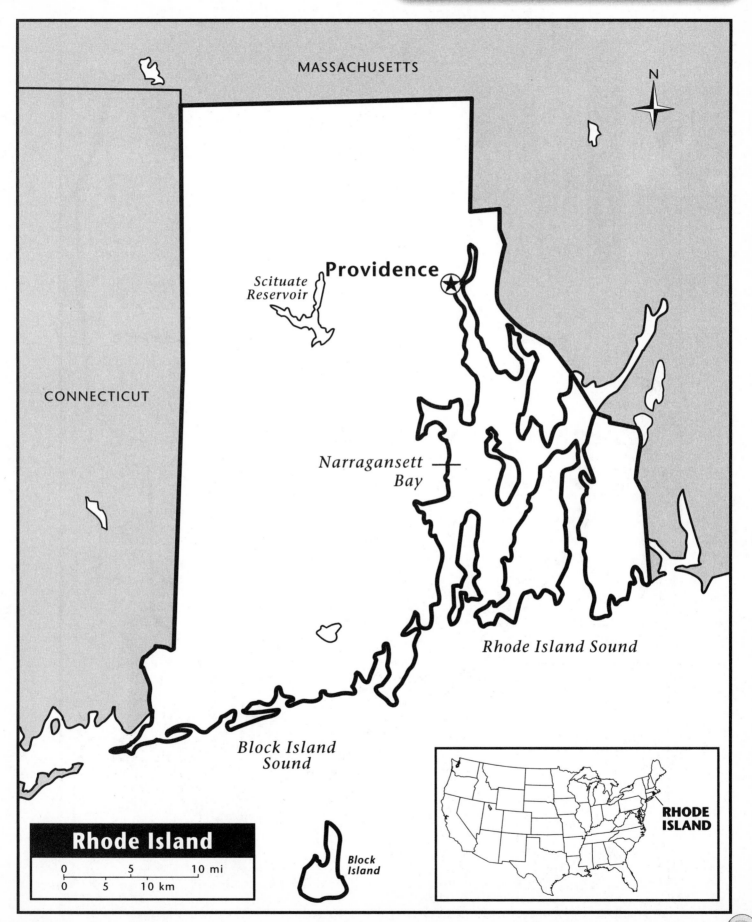

MASSACHUSETTS

N

CONNECTICUT

Providence

Scituate Reservoir

Narragansett Bay

Rhode Island Sound

Block Island Sound

Rhode Island

0   5   10 mi

0   5   10 km

Block Island

RHODE ISLAND

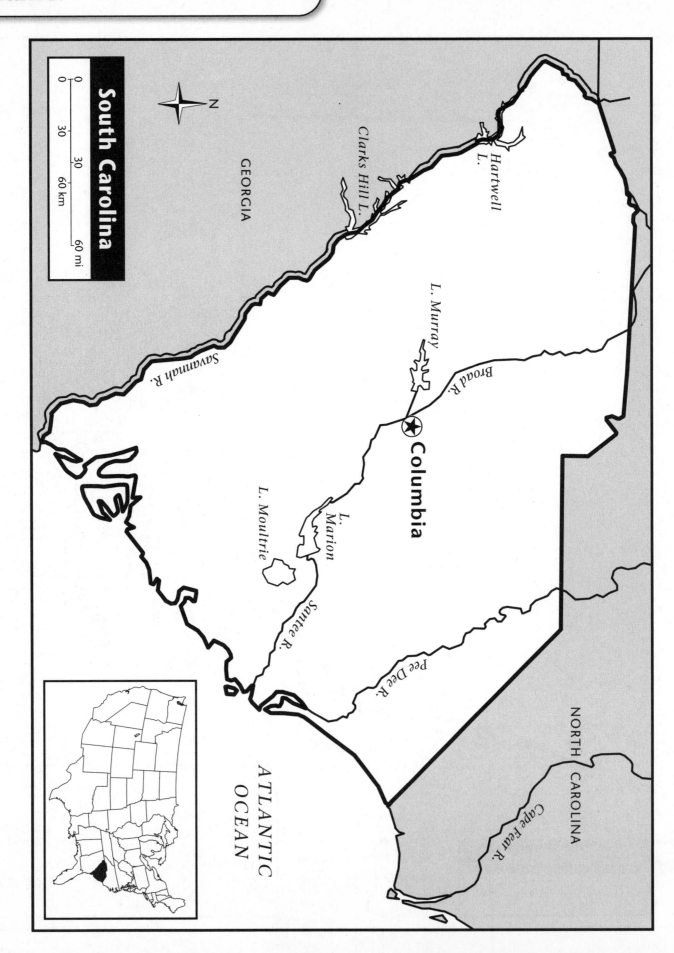

South Carolina

GEORGIA

Clarks Hill L.

Hartwell L.

L. Murray

Savannah R.

Broad R.

Columbia

L. Moultrie

L. Marion

Santee R.

Pee Dee R.

NORTH CAROLINA

Cape Fear R.

ATLANTIC OCEAN

0 30 60 km
0 30 60 mi

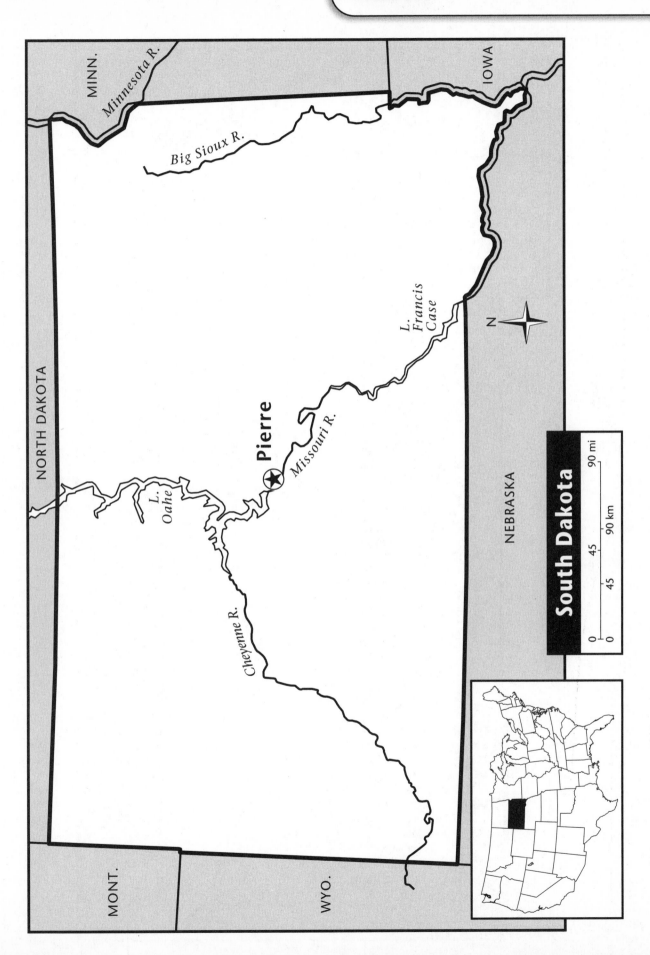

MINN.

Minnesota R.

IOWA

Big Sioux R.

N

L.
Francis
Case

NORTH DAKOTA

Pierre

Missouri R.

L.
Oahe

NEBRASKA

Cheyenne R.

South Dakota

90 mi

45

90 km

45

0

0

MONT.

WYO.

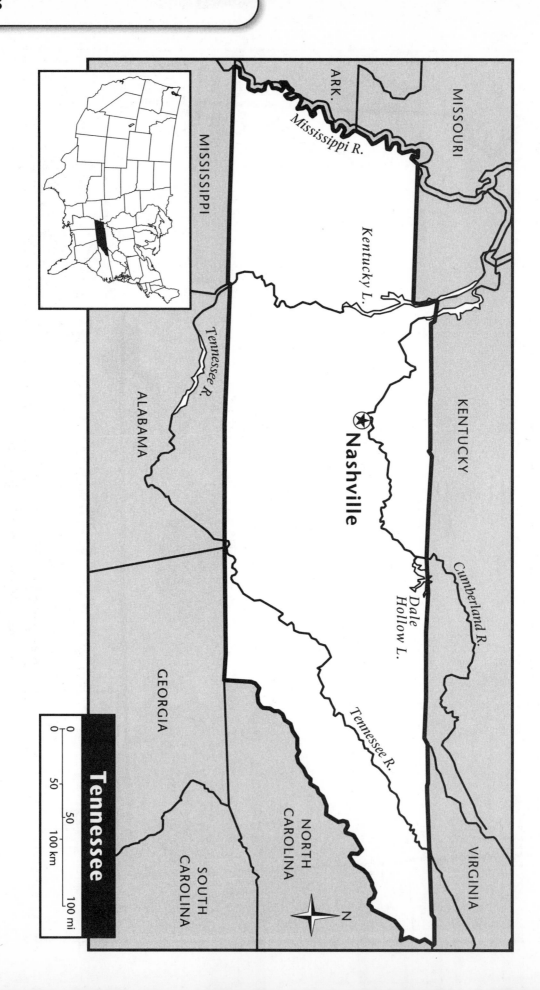

Tennessee

MISSISSIPPI

ARK.

MISSOURI

Mississippi R.

Kentucky L.

Tennessee R.

ALABAMA

KENTUCKY

⊛ Nashville

Dale Hollow L.

Cumberland R.

GEORGIA

Tennessee R.

NORTH CAROLINA

VIRGINIA

SOUTH CAROLINA

N

0 50 100 km
0 50 100 mi

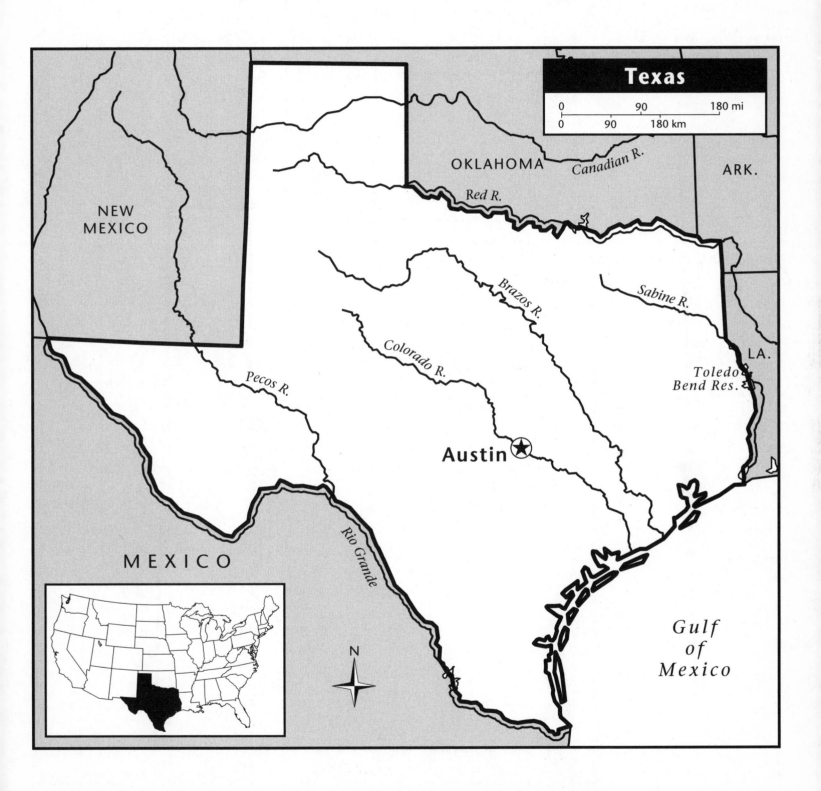

Texas

0   90   180 mi
0   90   180 km

NEW MEXICO

OKLAHOMA   Canadian R.   ARK.

Red R.

Brazos R.   Sabine R.

Colorado R.

LA.

Pecos R.   Toledo Bend Res.

Austin

Rio Grande

MEXICO

N

Gulf of Mexico

Name:

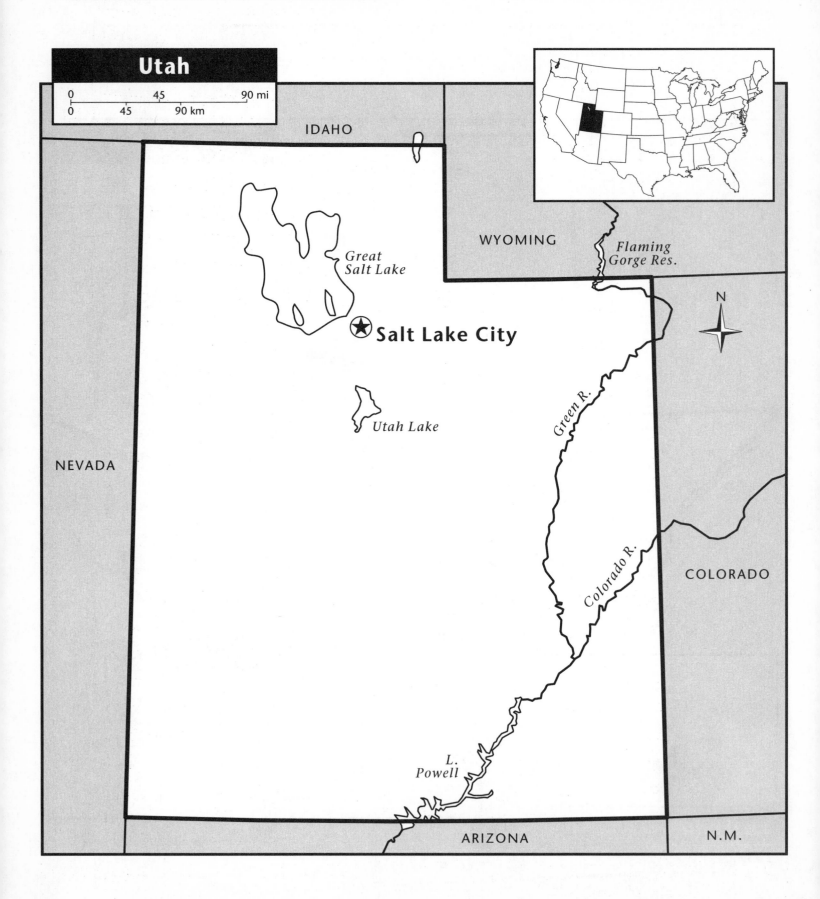

Utah

0   45   90 mi
0   45   90 km

IDAHO

WYOMING

Flaming Gorge Res.

Great Salt Lake

N

⭐ **Salt Lake City**

Utah Lake

NEVADA

Green R.

Colorado R.

COLORADO

L. Powell

ARIZONA

N.M.

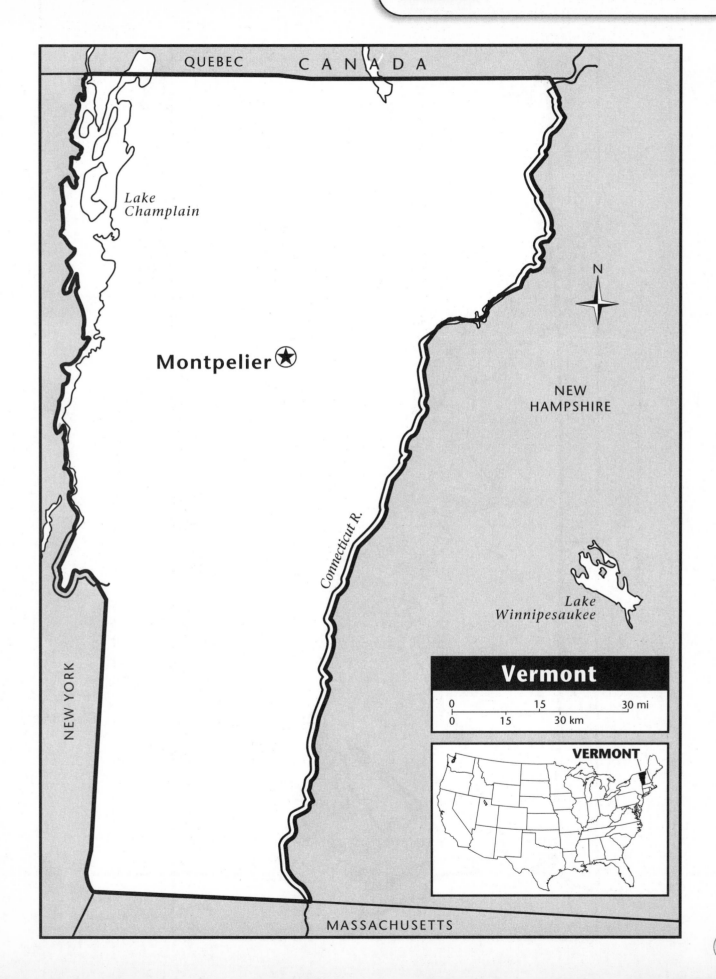

QUEBEC C A N A D A

Lake Champlain

Montpelier ★

N

NEW HAMPSHIRE

Connecticut R.

Lake Winnipesaukee

NEW YORK

Vermont

0   15   30 mi
0   15   30 km

VERMONT

MASSACHUSETTS

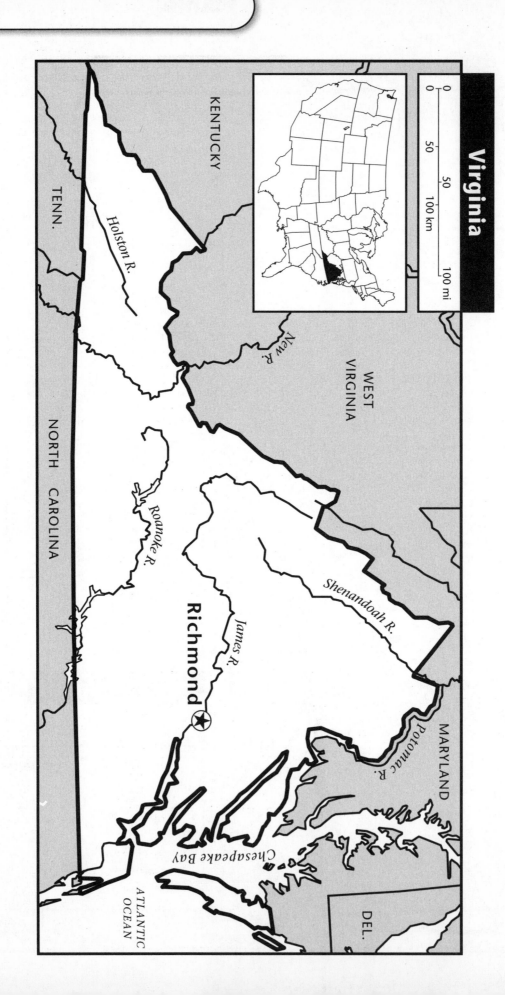

Name:

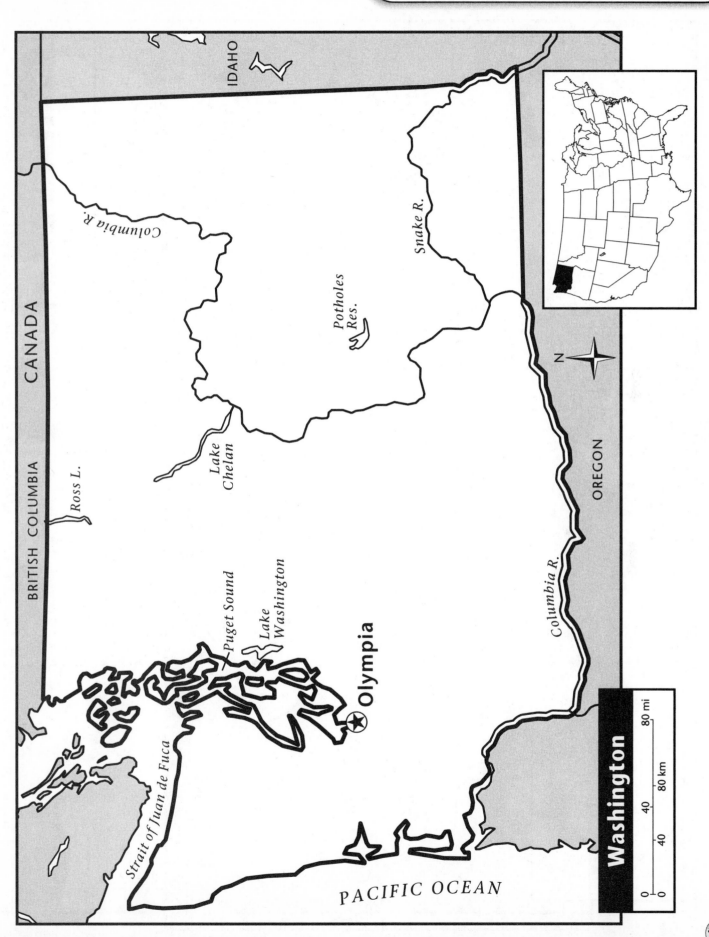

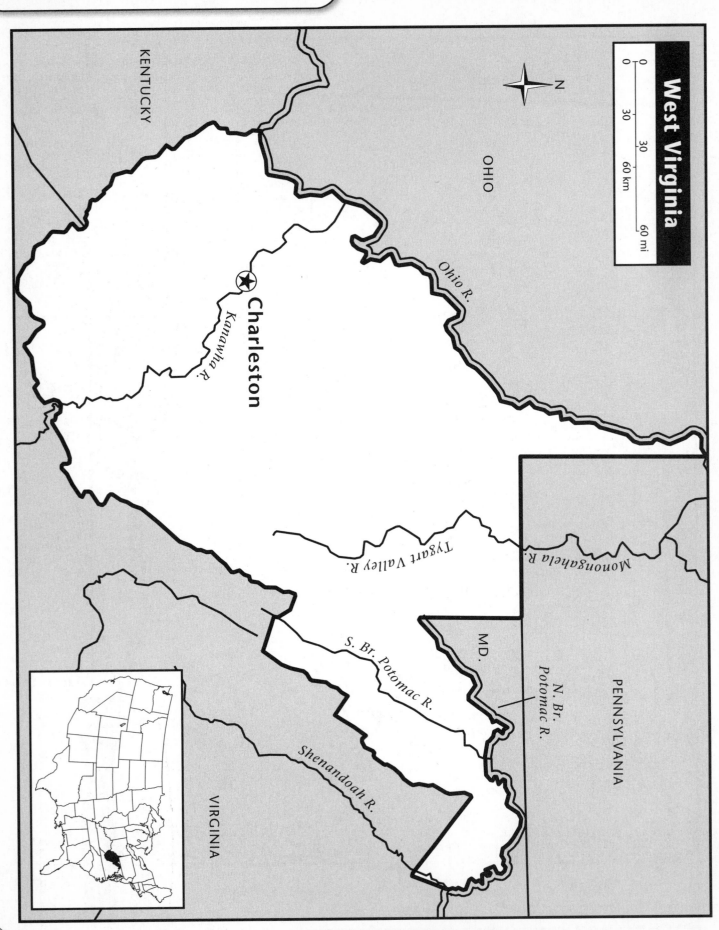

West Virginia

0
0
30
30
60 km
60 mi

N

KENTUCKY

OHIO

Ohio R.

Charleston

Kanawha R.

Tygart Valley R.

Monongahela R.

S. Br. Potomac R.

N. Br. Potomac R.

MD.

PENNSYLVANIA

Shenandoah R.

VIRGINIA

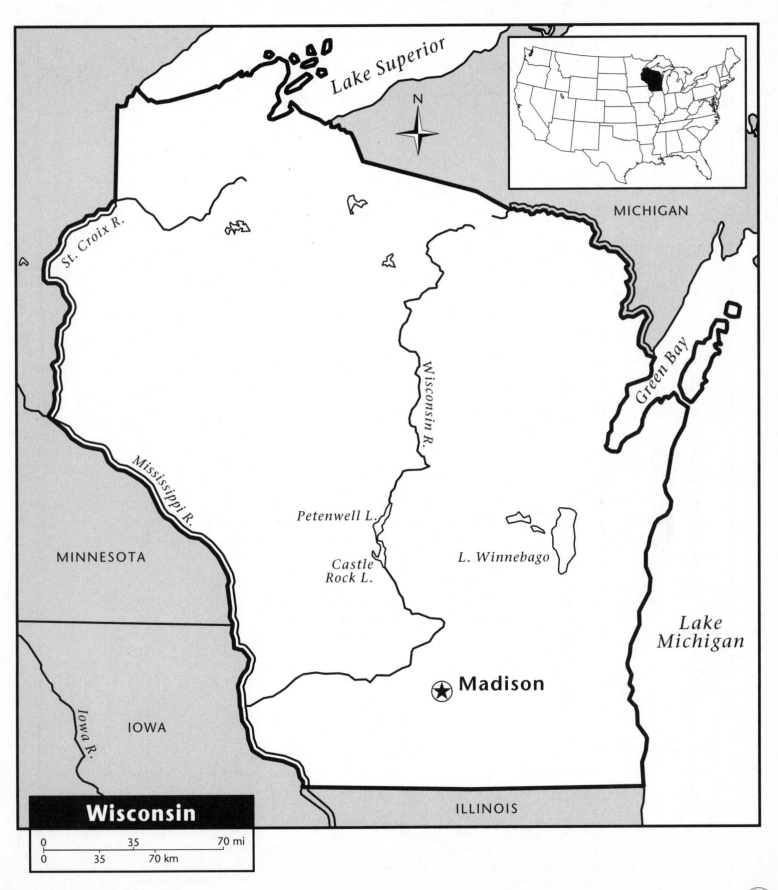

Lake Superior

N

MICHIGAN

St. Croix R.

Green Bay

Wisconsin R.

Mississippi R.

MINNESOTA

Petenwell L.

L. Winnebago

Castle
Rock L.

Lake
Michigan

★ **Madison**

Iowa R.

IOWA

ILLINOIS

Wisconsin

0	35	70 mi
0	35	70 km

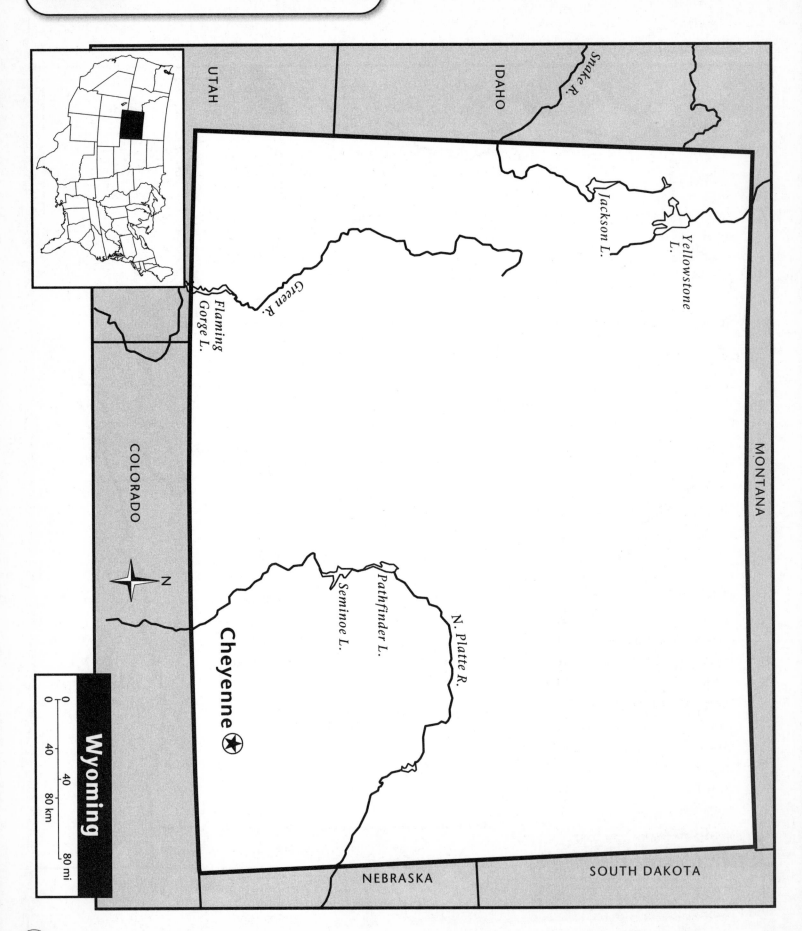

Name:

UTAH

IDAHO

Snake R.

Jackson L.

Yellowstone L.

MONTANA

Green R.

Flaming Gorge L.

COLORADO

N

Pathfinder L.

Seminoe L.

N. Platte R.

Cheyenne ✪

NEBRASKA

SOUTH DAKOTA

Wyoming

0   0
40 40
40 40
80 km 80 mi

Index